T

Our Father, Who ar[...]
Hallowed be Thy N[...]
Thy kingdom come.
Thy will be done on earth, as it is in heaven.
Give us this day our daily bread.
And forgive us our trespasses, as we forgive those who trespass against us.
And lead us not into temptation.
But deliver us from evil.
For Thine is the kingdom, and the power, and the glory, for ever and ever. Amen.

Part 4
The Sacrament of Baptism

"All authority hath been given unto Me in heaven and on earth. Go ye therefore, and make disciples of all the nations, baptizing them into the Name of the Father and of the Son and of the Holy Spirit; teaching them to observe all things whatsoever I commanded you."

Part 5
The Sacrament of the Altar

"Our Lord Jesus Christ, in the night in which He was betrayed, took bread; and when He had given thanks, He brake it and gave it to His disciples, saying, Take, eat; this is My Body, which is given for you; this do in remembrance of Me.

"After the same manner also He took the cup, when He had supped, and when He had given thanks, He gave it to them, saying, Drink ye all of it; this cup is the new testament in My Blood, which is shed for you, and for many, for the remission of sins; this do, as oft as ye drink it, in remembrance of Me."

The Senior Confirmation Book

A Mighty Fortress Is Our God

Martin Luther, 1529

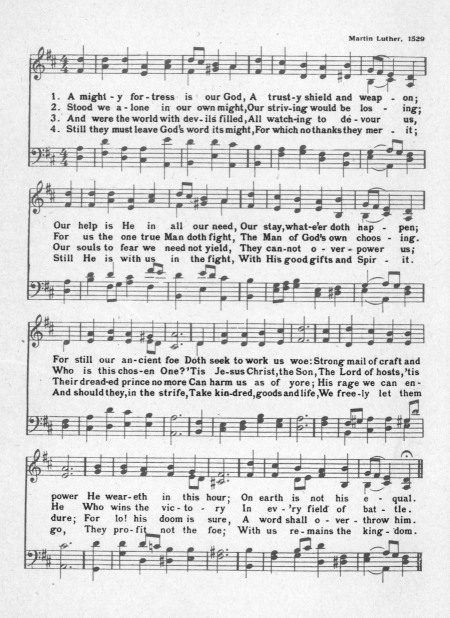

1. A might-y for-tress is our God, A trust-y shield and weap - on;
2. Stood we a-lone in our own might, Our striv-ing would be los - ing;
3. And were the world with dev-ils filled, All watch-ing to de - vour us,
4. Still they must leave God's word its might, For which no thanks they mer - it;

Our help is He in all our need, Our stay, what-e'er doth hap - pen;
For us the one true Man doth fight, The Man of God's own choos - ing.
Our souls to fear we need not yield, They can-not o - ver - power us;
Still He is with us in the fight, With His good gifts and Spir - it.

For still our an-cient foe Doth seek to work us woe: Strong mail of craft and
Who is this chos-en One? 'Tis Je-sus Christ, the Son, The Lord of hosts, 'tis
Their dread-ed prince no more Can harm us as of yore; His rage we can en-
And should they, in the strife, Take kin-dred, goods and life, We free-ly let them

power He wear-eth in this hour; On earth is not his e - qual.
He Who wins the vic-to - ry In ev - 'ry field of bat - tle.
dure; For lo! his doom is sure, A word shall o - ver - throw him.
go, They pro-fit not the foe; With us re-mains the king - dom.

THE SENIOR CONFIRMATION BOOK

by

JACOB TANNER

Issued under the auspices of
the Board of Parish Education

Published by

AUGSBURG PUBLISHING HOUSE
MINNEAPOLIS   MINNESOTA

THE SENIOR CONFIRMATION BOOK

Copyright 1941

Augsburg Publishing House

Manufactured in the United States of America

INTRODUCTION

PLAN

THE book is a course of instruction in God's way of salvation as outlined by the five parts of the Catechism. Brief summaries concluding the study of each part, serve as guides in the progress of the course. This arrangement also offers excellent opportunities for effective reviews.

PURPOSE

The book aims to furnish Christian nurture for baptized children.

SPECIAL FEATURES

1. In places, a brief historical background has been introduced. Our Christian faith has its roots in God's self-revelation from the garden of Eden to Christ. Christian faith is embedded in the process of history. Even a very limited knowledge of this fact has an inspiring effect.

2. The law was given to the Old Testament covenant people in order to teach them how they should live, to convict them of sin when they failed, and to make them realize their need of the promised Savior. It is this precedent that has caused a similar arrangement of the three uses of the law for the New Testament covenant people.

3. The discussion method has been chosen for the purpose of making the studies intelligible, personal, and interesting. An effort has been made to reach the hearts as well as the minds.

4. Following Luther, the discussion of the three Articles of Faith has retained the personal pronoun "I." Faith is a personal matter. The "I" is the reader, the one who makes

the confession, as is the case in the articles and in Luther's explanations. The same method is to some extent followed in other parts of the book.

USE

1. The passages to be memorized are printed in color. They consist of the Catechism text, Bible passages, and a few brief and simple definitions. The recitation of the memory work may be done at the beginning of the study of the lesson in class or at the close. It must not be overlooked.

2. The questions after each lesson should be answered in writing. *It is the main part of the pupils' home work and should be insisted upon.* By asking several pupils to read their answers to each question, it will be easy to check the work they are doing. The different answers will also offer opportunities for interesting and profitable discussions. The questions cover the lesson, and the answers are found in the lesson, requiring for the correct answer an intelligent study of the lesson. At the end of the class period the pastor should collect the papers and grade them, returning them at the next period. The benefits of this procedure are obvious.

3. The printed prayers may be used either at the beginning or at the conclusion of the study of the chapter. Let the class stand and, together with the pastor, pray the prayer, using their books. One pupil may also pray the prayer aloud while the others follow in their books. When the prayer consists of a hymn verse it should be sung by the class.

4. If we are to make our children more interested in and more at home with their Bible, the reading and underscoring of the passages in the Bible must become a regular practice as emphasized in the first item of the question lists. The students should bring their Bibles to every class. Where needed, Bibles may be furnished by some organization in the congregation, that will make it a special project to give well bound Bibles with cross-references to every incoming confirmation class.

5. The Bible Studies are related to the lesson material and are intended as home work for those who are able to handle additional work. All will benefit by the Bible Study work in class.

+   +

AN appeal to the parents seems a fitting conclusion to these introductory paragraphs. Take interest in the children's preparation for confirmation. Encourage and help them when needed. If you do not have family devotion, begin now. You cannot have a truly Christian home without God's Word and prayer. A Christian home is a part of the children's preparation for confirmation and for life.

+   +

MAY our God and Father in Jesus Christ accept *The Senior Confirmation Book* as a humble thank-offering for His unspeakable goodness. May its use be to the glory of His name and the coming of His kingdom.

THE AUTHOR.

TABLE OF CONTENTS

CHAPTER   PAGE

1   The Way of Salvation.....................................   1
2   The First Part or the Law............................   5
3   The First Commandment................................   9
4   The Second Commandment............................   13
5   The Third Commandment.............................   17
6   The Fourth Commandment...........................   22
7   The Fifth Commandment..............................   27
8   The Sixth Commandment   31
9   The Seventh Commandment   36
10 The Eighth Commandment............................   41
11 The Ninth and Tenth Commandments and the Conclusion 45
12 The Creed, and the Beginning of the First Article........   50
13 The First Article: God the Creator.......................   54
14 The First Article: God's Care for the World..............   58
15 The Second Article: Jesus Christ True God and True Man 62
16 The Second Article: The Redeemer......................   66
17 The Second Article: Jesus Christ the Suffering Savior......   70
18 The Second Article: Jesus Christ Risen from the Dead.....   74
19 The Second Article: Jesus Christ at the Right Hand of God 78
20 The Third Article: The Holy Spirit....................   82
21 The Third Article: The Holy Christian Church,
        the Communion of Saints............................   86
22 The Third Article: The Organized Church   90
23 The Third Article: The Forgiveness of Sin..............   96
24 The Third Article: The Holy Spirit Calls and Enlightens.100
25 The Third Article: Faith and Regeneration..............105
26 The Third Article: The Holy Spirit Sanctifies
        and Preserves 110
27 The Lord's Prayer: Introduction........................116
28 The First Three Petitions...............................120
29 The Fourth and Fifth Petitions.........................125
30 The Sixth and Seventh Petitions and the Conclusion......130
31 The Sacrament of Baptism.............................135
32 New Testament Baptism...............................140
33 Infant Baptism 146
34 The Sacrament of the Altar: Confession.................152
35 The Sacrament of the Altar: Benefits...................158
36 Old Truths and New Experiences.....................163

CHAPTER ONE

The Way of Salvation

IN THE NAME OF JESUS CHRIST

It is God's will that all men be saved and come to the knowledge of the truth **(I Tim. 2:4)**.

The purpose of this course is to acquaint every student with God's way of salvation so that he might walk in it.

1. SALVATION COMES FROM GOD

When Adam and Eve had sinned, they hid themselves for they were afraid of God. It was God who came to them; they did not go to God. God, not man, planned our salvation and sent Jesus Christ to be our Savior.

For God so loved the world, that He gave His only begotten Son, that whosoever believeth on Him should not perish, but have eternal life **(John 3:16)**.

2. THE BIBLE

God has given us the Bible in order that we may learn to know Jesus Christ, believe on Him, and have life eternal.

These are written, that ye may believe that Jesus is the Christ, the Son of God, and that believing ye may have life in His name **(John 20:31)**.

The Bible was written during a period of about 1600 years, from 1500 B. C. to 100 A. D. It is divided into the Old Testament, containing thirty-nine books, and the New Testament, containing twenty-seven books—sixty-six books in all.

The Old Testament covers the time from creation to about 400 B. C. It tells how God, through the people of Israel, prepared for the coming of Jesus Christ. The New Testament books begin with the coming of Christ and were completed not later than the year 100.

For the writing of the Bible, God used prophets in the Old Testament and evangelists and apostles in the New Testament.[1] These men were instructed and guided by the Holy Spirit to understand what God said and did and to use the right words when telling it to others. The Bible is, therefore, verbally inspired of God.

No prophecy ever came by the will of man, but men spake from God, being moved by the Holy Spirit (II Peter 1:21).

3. LAW AND GOSPEL

The Bible consists of law and gospel.

The law tells us what we must do and what we must not do.

The gospel is the good news of salvation from sin through Jesus Christ.

Both law and gospel are found in the Old Testament as well as in the New. It is in Exodus, chapter 20, that we have the Ten Commandments. In the Sermon on the Mount, Matt. 5 to 7, Christ explains the law. The first gospel message is in Genesis 3:15. Isaiah 53 is another gospel message in the Old Testament. The New Testament is full of the good news of Jesus Christ, the Savior.

Wherever the Bible is used and believed, the Holy Spirit creates a new and better life. Purity, honesty, justice, and love take the place of impurity, dishonesty, injustice, and hatred.

The gospel is the power of God unto salvation to every one that believeth (Rom. 1:16).

All Scripture is given by inspiration of God, and is profitable for doctrine, for reproof, for correction, for instruction in righteousness (II Tim. 3:16; Authorized Version).

---

[1]By prophets we mean all the men God used to write the Old Testament. We know the names of most of these men. Evangelists and apostles were the men who wrote the New Testament. We call the men who wrote the four Gospels evangelists, though two of them, Matthew and John, were apostles.

The Bible has by now, as a whole or in parts, been translated into more than a thousand different languages and dialects.

4. BAPTISM AND INSTRUCTION

In order to be saved from sin we must be made disciples of Christ according to His command:

Go ye and make disciples of all the nations, baptizing them into the name of the Father and of the Son and of the Holy Spirit, teaching them to observe all things whatsoever I commanded you (Matt. 28:19-20) .

In obedience to this command of Christ's you have been baptized and instructed in His Word.

5. THE CATECHISM

Luther's Small Catechism has been one of your main books of instruction. The Catechism is a simple and brief summary of the teachings of the Bible. It was written by Martin Luther in 1529 and has been translated into more than 150 languages and dialects. As the Lutheran Church goes into new mission fields, Luther's Small Catechism is translated into still more languages.

The Catechism is divided into five parts:

The first part: The Ten Commandments or the Law.

The second part: The Creed or the Christian Faith.

The third part: The Lord's Prayer.

The fourth part: The Sacrament of Baptism.

The fifth part: The Sacrament of the Lord's Supper

The last four parts contain the gospel.

The book you now are going to study is an explanation of the Bible truth as taught in the Catechism.

Prayer:
> Precious Jesus, I beseech Thee:
> May Thy words take root in me;
> May this gift from heaven enrich me,
> So that I bear fruit for Thee;
> Take them never from my heart
> Till I see Thee as Thou art,
> When in heavenly bliss and glory
> I shall see Thee and adore Thee. Amen.
> (L. H. No. 260, v. 4)

QUESTIONS
(To be answered in writing, except 1 and 2)

1. Look up and read in your Bible the Bible passages quoted in this chapter. Underscore them in your Bible. *(The Bible passages are printed in italics in all lessons.)*

2. Be ready to recite the material that is to be memorized. *It is printed in green in every chapter.*

3. What did Adam and Eve do when they had sinned?

4. With whom did man's salvation have its beginning?

5. Write John 3:16 from memory.

6. Why did God give us the Bible?

7. During what time was the Bible written?

8. Who wrote the Bible?

9. How could men's writings be God's Word?

10. What do we mean when we say that the Bible is verbally inspired?

11. What is the message of the Old Testament?

12. And of the New Testament?

13. What is the law?

14. What is the gospel?

15. Describe the influence of the Bible where it is believed and used.

16. Why have you been baptized and instructed in the Word of God?

17. When was your Small Catechism written? By whom?

18. Into how many parts is it divided?

19. Write the names of the parts of the Catechism.

20. State the purpose of this course of study.

BIBLE STUDY

1. How many books are there in the Old Testament? In the New Testament? How many in the whole Bible?

2. Write the names of the books of the Bible in the proper order.

CHAPTER TWO

The First Part or the Law

If we are to understand the place of the law in God's plan of salvation, we must take a look at God's covenant, for the law is a part of the covenant.

1. THE COVENANT

A covenant is a contract that guarantees the fulfillment of what has been promised. God made a covenant with Noah and put the rainbow in the sky as a sign or a token that He would fulfill the promise (Gen. 9:8-17). Again God entered into a covenant with Abraham and made circumcision the sign of the covenant (Gen. 17:1-14).

At Sinai God entered into a covenant with His people Israel. He pledged Himself to be their God and to make them a holy people whom He would use to bring salvation to all mankind. The people pledged themselves to trust God and keep His word. This covenant was sealed with blood, called the blood of the covenant (Ex. 24:3-8).

God has also made His covenant with His new testament people. This covenant He made with each one when we were baptized. God pledged Himself to forgive our sins and to be our Father in Christ Jesus and we pledged that we would believe in Him and forsake the devil. This covenant too is sealed with blood, the blood of Jesus Christ.

If we ask what moved God to enter into a covenant with His people, there is only one answer, His love.

5

2. THE MEANS OF GRACE

We have learned that the covenant is God's guaranty that He will fulfill His promises. He has promised to save sinners and He is working at it all the time. He teaches us how to live, He opens our eyes to see that we are sinners, He offers forgiveness of sin through the Savior, and He leads us to faith in Jesus Christ and to a God-fearing life. The means God uses in this work are called the means of grace. They are the Word and the Sacraments. Through these means God gives the grace that we need in order to be saved.

The law is a part of God's Word. The love that moved God to give us the gospel also moved Him to give us His holy law. Without the work of the law no one would accept Christ as his personal Savior.

At Sinai God introduced the lawgiving in these words: "I am the Lord thy God, who brought thee out of the land of Egypt, out of the house of bondage" (Ex. 20:2). What God had done for them proved that He loved them, and because He loved them, He would now give them His law.

3. THE LAW

We shall now begin a study of the law; but let us first pray, O God my Father, teach me to know and to love Thy law. Amen.

God first inscribed His law in the heart of man at creation; later He gave the Ten Commandments on two tables or tablets of stone at Mount Sinai.

The law inscribed in our hearts we call the conscience.

The Gentiles show the work of the law written in their hearts, their conscience bearing witness therewith (Rom. 2:15).

The conscience is always on the side of what we believe to be right. Since the Fall it has been darkened because man's understanding was darkened. Unless instructed by the Word of God, the conscience may be on the side of what is wrong, because we believe it to be right. In order that we may know what is right, God has given us the written law.

Jesus divided the law into two parts—love to God and love to man (Matt. 22:37-39). The first three commandments teach love to God and the last seven love to our neighbor. It is this division the church followed when plac-

6

ing the first three commandments in the first table and the last seven in the second.

Thou shalt love the Lord thy God with all thy heart, and with all thy soul, and with all thy mind. This is the great and first commandment. And a second like unto it is this, Thou shalt love thy neighbor as thyself (Matt. 22: 37-39).

Love is the fulfillment of the law (Rom. 13:10).

4. THE PURPOSE OF THE LAW

God gave the law for a threefold purpose:

I. To teach His people how to live;

II. To convince us that we are sinners;

III. To drive us to Christ.

Let us briefly look at each of these three purposes.

I. Through the law God teaches His people how to live.

The commandment is a lamp; and the law is light (Prov. 6:23).

God's law is not a number of burdensome rules given for the purpose of making life hard for us. The commandments are markers that tell where the highway of life runs. In the commandments our heavenly Father comes and, taking us by the hand, He invites us to walk through life together with Him.

Jesus Christ is also in the company explaining and illustrating by His life and His words what the commandments mean. For He fulfilled every one of them.

Thus, the child of God learns how he should live.

II. The law convinces us that we are sinners.

As we travel along in this company, we gradually learn that we too often think, say, and do that which is not right. Then the law condemns us, the conscience accuses us, and we are unhappy.

Through the law cometh the knowledge of sin (Rom. 3:20).

III. The law drives us to Christ.

When we realize that we have failed, we try to do better. If we are in earnest, we put all our energy and will power into the task of improving ourselves. And then something unexpected happens. In spite of our most intense efforts we are unable to produce the love to God and to man and the purity of heart that God demands of us in His law.

7

Only the forgiveness of sin can remove the condemnation of the law and can still our conscience. And forgiveness of sin is the gift of Jesus Christ.

The law is become our tutor to bring us unto Christ (Gal. 3:24).

Prayer:

My God and Father, I thank Thee for giving me a conscience and for the light of Thy law. Give me Thy Holy Spirit that I may come to know Thy holy will as I study Thy law. Help me to be an obedient child of Thine. In Christ my Lord. Amen.

WORD STUDY

Condemnation: pronouncing of judgment. Tutor: a private instructor.

QUESTIONS
(To be answered in writing, except 1 and 2)

1. Look up and read in your Bible the Bible passages quoted in this chapter. Underscore them in your Bible.
2. Be ready to recite the material that is to be memorized.
3. What is a covenant?
4. Why did God enter into covenants with man?
5. With whom did God establish His covenant at Mt. Sinai?
6. What did God pledge?
7. What did the people pledge?
8. When did God enter into a covenant with you?
9. What pledge did God make? And you?
10. What is a means of grace?
11. Name the means of grace.
12. Explain the relation between God's covenant and the means of grace.
13. What moved God to give man His law?
14. Explain the relation between the written law and the conscience.
15. Why may the conscience approve what is wrong?
16. In what two commandments did Christ summarize the whole law?
17. What is the threefold purpose of the law?
18. Of what benefit is this lesson to you?

BIBLE STUDY

1. Read Gen. 9:8-17 and point out (1) with whom God here entered into a covenant; (2) what God pledged; and (3) the sign of the covenant.
2. After reading Ex. 24:3-8 point out (1) the people's answer to the ordinances that Moses brought them; (2) what Moses did with the blood he put into basins (compare verses 6 and 8); (3) what is called the book of the covenant (compare verses 4 and 7); (4) the meaning of the term "the blood of the covenant."

CHAPTER THREE

THE INTRODUCTION
I am the Lord thy God.

The First Commandment

Thou shalt have no other gods before Me.

What is meant by this?

Answer: We should fear, love, and trust in God above all things.

1. THE SPEAKER

It is God, your heavenly Father, who speaks in the commandments.

He uses the word "thou" because He speaks to each one of us, to you and to me.

Hear, O heavens, and give ear, O earth; for the Lord hath spoken (Is. 1:2).

The Jewish teachers at the time of Christ taught the law in a manner that was contrary to God's word in the Old Testament. In the Sermon on the Mount and on other occasions Christ gave the true meaning of the law and its application to our daily life. Luther explained the commandments in the light of the teachings of Christ.

Studying the commandments in this light, we see that each commandment speaks of the evil we must not do and of the good we must do.

2. WORSHIP OF IDOLS FORBIDDEN

In the First Commandment God forbids us to love and serve other gods or idols.[1]

Idolatry—the worship of many gods—was Israel's national sin for a thousand years. The people learned it in Egypt, and neither kindness nor punishment could break them away from it till the nation was utterly ruined and carried away into Babylonian captivity.

God must have the first place in the heart and whatever takes His place becomes an idol. Of the strange gods served even in Christendom money, power, fashions are some of the most common.

Idol worship in any form stirs up the evil desires in man and makes a holy life impossible. Pride, hatred, greed, injustice, fear are some of its fruits. As long as man serves idols, Christ Jesus cannot come in. Either idol worship must be rooted out or man must perish.

My beloved, flee from idolatry (I Cor. 10:14).

Thou shalt worship the Lord thy God, and Him only shalt thou serve (Matt. 4:10).

Jesus Christ is the only Mediator between God and man. It is contrary to the Word of God to pray to Mary and other saints, asking them to pray to God for us. The saints were saved by the same grace as the rest of us. They have no other standing before God and no other influence than every other saved soul. The practice comes under idolatry.

3. FEAR, LOVE, AND TRUST COMMANDED

According to the First Commandment we should fear, love, and trust in God above all things. This is what God wants you and me to do. Let us see if we can probe a little deeper into these words as we apply them to ourselves.

I. The Fear of God. As good children have reverence and respect for their father and obey him, so God's children have reverence and respect for their heavenly Father and obey Him.

---

[1] It has been an almost universal practice to make images of the godhead. People believed that the deity lived in the image. By worshipping the image they worshipped the deity. That was what the Israelites did when they made a golden calf and worshipped it (Ex. 32:1-6). In order to make clear that such practices were contrary to the First Commandment, God added: "Thou shalt not make unto thee a graven image, nor any likeness of anything that is in heaven above, or that is in the earth beneath, or that is in the water under the earth; thou shalt not bow down thyself unto them, nor serve them" (Ex. 20:4-5).

We fear God when we show Him reverence, respect, and obedience. This is called filial fear. Joseph's answer reveals the right fear of God: *How can I do this great wickedness, and sin against God?* (Gen. 39:9.)

There are some children who have no respect for their father and are as disobedient as they dare to be and still escape punishment. There are many people who treat God in the same way. They fear only the punishment. This is called slavish fear.

Some people are much more afraid of what others will say, or do, than they are of God. They become the slaves of comrades, voters, and fashions and are idol worshippers.

If God is for us, who is against us? (Rom. 8:31.)

II. The Love of God. You cannot produce love by commanding another to love you. Only love creates love.

God loved you before you were born. Life, family, friends, school, work, fun, the privilege of being God's children, and the daily forgiveness of sin are gifts by which God shows that He loves you. And then He established His covenant of love with you in Baptism. He even loves the ungodly.

Do not accept God's gifts thoughtlessly. What do these and many other blessings mean in your life? Ask the Holy Spirit to help you to appreciate God's great and undeserved goodness to you. And there will be love of God in your heart.

We love, because He first loved us (I John 4:19).

Love must be active in obedience, otherwise your love will die. Love and disobedience cannot go together.

Jesus said: *If ye love Me, ye will keep My commandments* (John 14:15)

III. The Trust in God. We trust those whom we find trustworthy and on whom we can depend. Our heavenly Father is trustworthy and we can depend upon Him.

God is not a man, that He should lie. . . . Hath He said, and will He not do it? Or hath He spoken, and will He not make it good? (Num. 23:19).

4. GOD WILLING AND ABLE TO HELP

No one has such a Father as God's children have. He is both ready and able to help us.

Behold, the Lord's hand is not shortened, that He cannot save (Is. 59:1).

Prayer:

Dear Lord Jesus Christ, I thank Thee for the example of Thy life. I confess that I have not feared, loved, and trusted my heavenly Father as I should and ask forgiveness for my sin. Inspire and strengthen me ever to become more like Thee.

> The dearest idol I have known,
> Whate'er that idol be,
> Help me to tear it from Thy throne,
> And worship only Thee. Amen.
>
> (L. H. No. 501, v. 3.)

WORD STUDY

Mediator: one who intercedes or pleads in behalf of another.

Filial: as befits a child, child-like, "sonly."

QUESTIONS
(To be answered in writing, except 1 and 2)

1. Look up and read in your Bible the Bible passages quoted in this chapter. Underscore them in your Bible.
2. Be ready to recite the material that is to be memorized.
3. What made it necessary for Christ to explain the true meaning of God's law?
4. On whose teaching are Luther's explanations of the commandments based?
5. What is the evil forbidden in the First Commandment?
6. What is the good this commandment instructs us to do?
7. What place should God have in your heart and life?
8. Name some idols served in so-called Christian lands.
9. Describe some of the effects of idol worship.
10. Explain "filial fear."
11. Explain "slavish fear."
12. What kind of fear of God should a Christian have?
13. Why should we love God above all things?
14. How should our love of God show itself in our daily life?
15. How can you and I acquire such love of God?
16. Why should we trust in God?
17. From the Old Testament, name a person who feared, loved, and trusted God.
18. What impression has this lesson made upon you?

BIBLE STUDY

1. Read Ps. 115:2-8 and point out the contrast between Jehovah and the idols.
2. After reading Mark 12:41-44 point out (1) the difference between the gifts of the others and the gift of the widow; (2) what Jesus said of the widow's gift; (3) what in your judgment moved the widow to bring her gift.
3. How would you like to be examined the way the man was of whom we read in John 21:15-19?

CHAPTER FOUR

The Second Commandment

Thou shalt not take the name of the Lord thy God in vain; for the Lord will not hold him guiltless that taketh His name in vain.

What does this mean?

Answer: We should fear and love God so that we do not curse, swear, conjure, lie or deceive by His name, but call upon Him in every time of need, and worship Him with prayer, praise, and thanksgiving.

1. A GOOD AND HONORABLE FATHER

God is a good and honorable father. "He maketh His sun to rise on the evil and the good, and sendeth rain on the just and the unjust" (Matt. 5:45). If He should withhold His blessings we would all perish. And He sent His son to save us from eternal destruction!

It is a terrible testimony to the wickedness of man that people use God's name without respect and for evil purposes, and do it without any sense of shame.

2. MISUSING GOD'S NAME

God gave the commandments for our sake. In each commandment He guards something that is of the greatest importance for our welfare. In the Second Commandment He guards against the misuse of His name. Nothing is more important for our welfare than God's name.

If you use God's name without respect, you have no respect for God. He has no place in your thinking, no place in your conscience. Your conversation has no room for God, and in your life He is an outsider. God can get along without you, but how would you fare without Him?

If God has no place in your life, you have no one to go to in trouble, no one to help you in temptation, no one to forgive your sins, give your conscience peace, and put you on your feet again. You have no one to keep alive a saving faith and to light a dying hour. Misusing God's name drives God out of your life. It is a most serious sin.

Thou shalt not take the name of the Lord thy God in vain (Ex. 20:7).

3. CURSE NOT

"We should fear and love God so that we do not curse, swear, conjure, lie, or deceive by His name."

I. People who curse and swear find in this sin an outlet for uncontrolled anger or meanness, or they do it because it has become a habit with them.

Bless, and curse not (Rom. 12:14).

II. The more people lose faith in God's Word the more will conjuring and other superstitious and evil practices flourish.

Whosoever doeth these things is an abomination unto the Lord (Deut. 18:12)

III. People who pervert God's Word by false teaching and those who pretend to be Christians but are hypocrites, lie and deceive by God's name. It is a sad fact that Christendom is full of such liars and deceivers.

This people honoreth Me with their lips; but their heart is far from Me (Matt. 15:8).

Let us again repeat what God says of those who commit such evils: "The Lord will not hold him guiltless that taketh His name in vain" (Ex. 20:7).

4. THE OATH

Though the Word of God forbids swearing, it makes one exception. A Christian may be sworn as an officer of the law or as a witness. Christ Himself testified when the high priest appealed to Him under oath (Matt. 26:63-64).

It is the government's duty to administer the laws righteously in order that all may have justice. For this purpose the government must make sure that officials perform their

14

duties faithfully and that witnesses testify truthfully. A solemn oath administered by a judge or another official is used for this purpose.

Still, such an oath is of value only when people fear and respect God. Where this fear and respect are lost, there will be just as much lying under oath as without it. The result is perjury in court cases which is sin both against God and society.

Ye shall not swear by My name falsely, and profane the name of thy God; I am the Lord (Lev. 19:12).

5. THE USE OF GOD'S NAME

"We should fear and love God so that we ... call upon Him in every time of need, and worship Him with prayer, praise, and thanksgiving."

I. Luther's explanations of this and the following commandments begin, "We should fear and love God." The reason is that only those who fear and love God can do IIis will.

If a person tries to obey God simply as a matter of duty, he will soon tire. Only he to whom the commandments are his heavenly Father's will, loves to obey. He alone is sorry enough to ask forgiveness when he has failed. Only in such a heart can the Holy Spirit renew fear and love of God.

II. Calling upon God's name. We need God and He wants to take care of us. He invites us to bring our needs and troubles to Him.

Call upon Me in the day of trouble; I will deliver thee, and thou shalt glorify Me (Ps. 50:15).

III. Worshiping God. It is a glorious privilege to have a Father in heaven whom we can call upon and who is always ready to listen and to help. Let us worship Him with prayer, praise, and thanksgiving.

Oh give thanks unto the Lord; for He is good; for His lovingkindness endureth forever (Ps. 106:1).

Prayer:

Thy name, O Lord, abideth,
Thou shalt be honored on the earth,
Thy hand our all provideth,
Thou carest for us ere our birth.
O Lord! What shall we render
For all the debt we owe,

For all Thy care so tender,
Thy love too vast to know?
The theme of Thy salvation
Shall be our one employ,
We bless Thee for creation,
And for eternal joy. Amen.

(L. H. No. 385, v. 3)

15

WORD STUDY

Take in vain: misuse, use without respect or for evil purposes. Conjure: use sorcery, witchcraft, or magic. Abomination: something to be abhorred, detested. Pervert: falsify. Perjury: wilful false statement under oath. Worship: render reverence, give honor, adore.

QUESTIONS
(To be answered in writing, except 1 and 2)

1. Look up and read in your Bible the Bible passages quoted in this chapter. Underscore them in your Bible.
2. Be ready to recite the material that is to be memorized.
3. What evil is forbidden in the Second Commandment?
4. Explain the meaning of "take in vain."
5. State how God shows that He is a good and honorable Father.
6. How would you feel if some one misused your father's name the way people misuse God's name?
7. Why has God, in the Second Commandment, guarded His name against misuse?
8. What effect does "taking God's name in vain" have upon a person?
9. According to the explanation to the Second Commandment, in what ways is God's name taken in vain?
10. Why do people curse and swear?
11. State what God's Word says about cursing.
12. State what God's Word says about conjuring and other superstitious practices.
13. According to God's Word, what is wrong with the people who profess God's name though they are hypocrites?
14. What does God mean when He says that He will not hold him guiltless who takes His name in vain?
15. For what purpose is the oath used by the government?
16. Why is the oath often without any value?
17. If we do not fear and love God we cannot do His will. Why not?
18. What does the Second Commandment instruct us to do?
19. Why does God invite us to call upon Him in our troubles?
20. Why should we worship God with prayer, praise, and thanksgiving?
21. Applying this commandment to yourself, are you satisfied with yourself?

BIBLE STUDY

1. After reading Job 3:1; II Sam. 16:5-8; and Matt. 26:74, state how each of these men profaned God's name.
2. What two persons in Luke, chapter 2, worshipped God with praise and thanksgiving?
3. In Acts 16:23-25 we are told that Paul and Silas had been beaten and cast into prison where they sang hymns unto God. Can you give any reason why they should sing hymns?

16

CHAPTER FIVE

The Third Commandment

Remember the Sabbath day, to keep it holy.

What does this mean?

Answer: We should fear and love God so that we do not despise His Word and the preaching of the same,[1] but deem it holy, and gladly hear and learn it.

1. THE OLD TESTAMENT DAY OF REST

Sabbath means rest. Saturday, the seventh day of the week, was the day of rest in the Old Testament.

God gave the Sabbath to Israel for a double purpose. It was to be a day of rest (Ex. 20:9-10), and a day of public worship (Lev. 23:3). The Sabbath day was a day of refreshing for body and soul, a gift of love to the people.

Six days thou shalt do thy work, and on the seventh day thou shalt rest (Ex. 23:12).

The seventh day Sabbath belongs to the Old Testament system just as do circumcision, the priesthood, the sacrifices, and the temple.[2] They were all a part of the prepara-

---

[1] Luther's words are: so we do not despise preaching and His Word.

[2] In Ex. 31:16-17 we read that the Sabbath is to be "a perpetual covenant," "a sign for ever." Gen. 17:13 states that circumcision is "for an everlasting covenant." Ex. 40:15 informs us that the Aaronic priesthood is "an everlasting priesthood"; and Lev. 16:34 says that the law about the national sacrifice on the Day of Atonement should be "an everlasting statute." Perpetual, for ever, and everlasting mean the same. If the seventh day Sabbath were binding in the New Testament, so would circumcision, the Aaronic priesthood, and the annual sacrifice on the Day of Atonement be. According to the law of Moses, these were no less everlasting than the seventh day Sabbath. As all these institutions belonged to the Old Testament covenant, so they should be in force forever within the covenant, that is, as long as the covenant lasted. When the covenant came to an end at the coming of Christ, the different parts of it also came to an end. Circumcision, the Aaronic priesthood, sacrifices, and the Old Testament Sabbath day have no part or place in the New Testament covenant.

tion for the coming of Christ. At His coming their usefulness came to an end, for in Him they were fulfilled. The
Sabbath pointed forward to Christ in whom the believers
find rest for their souls. The Sabbath is, therefore, called a
shadow of the things to come.

*Let no man therefore judge you in meat, or in drink, or
in respect of a feast day or a new moon or a sabbath day:
which are a shadow of the things to come* (Col. 2:16-17).

2. SUNDAY OUR DAY OF REST

All days are equally holy unto God. We should use God's
Word and glorify and serve the Lord every day of the week.

However, the New Testament church needed a day
when the congregation could come together for public worship. The church could have chosen any day, but Sunday
was agreed upon because in a special sense it was the Lord's
day. On a Sunday Christ rose from the dead (Easter Sunday), and on a Sunday the Holy Spirit was poured out and
the church was born (Pentecost Sunday). The result was
that Sunday was called the Lord's day and was selected as
the day for public worship.

This practice started during the lifetime of the apostles
and, of course, with their approval. We can see the beginning of this development in Acts 20:7; I Cor. 16:2; and
Rev. 1:10.

In order to make it possible for the congregation to come
together to hear God's Word on Sunday, the day had to be
a day of rest from everyday work and duties. In this way
Sunday, to the Christians, became the day of rest and of
public worship. As Christianity spread, this use of the
Lord's day became the accepted order.

3. THE PURPOSE OF THE CHRISTIAN SUNDAY

The purpose of the Christian Sunday is to provide an
opportunity for coming together to hear God's Word.
Where God's Word is being preached in truth and purity,
there God meets His people and the people worship God.

The fact that Sunday became a day of rest in order to
make regular public worship possible has also brought us
physical and social blessings. By setting aside one day a
week for bodily rest and recuperation and for the coming
together of family and friends, our health is protected and

maintained and family ties and friendships may be cultivated and made more valuable.

For most of us Sunday also offers a better opportunity than the weekdays for visiting the sick, the shut-ins, the prisoners, and others who are in need of bodily or spiritual help, or both.

Pure religion and undefiled before our God and Father is this, to visit the fatherless and widows in their affliction, and to keep oneself unspotted from the world (James 1:27).

Since Sunday brings so many opportunities and blessings, the misuse of the day becomes a serious sin.

4. THE MISUSE OF THE DAY OF REST

We misuse the Sunday when we make light of the preaching of God's Word, stay away from church services on a poor excuse or for no reason at all, and fail to use the day for spiritual and physical refreshing.

A Christian should watch over his Sunday and not permit Sunday papers, social gatherings and the like to rob him of the blessings of the day of rest and public worship.

Let us consider one another to provoke unto love and good works; not forsaking our own assembling together, as the custom of some is (Heb. 10:24-25).

5. KEEPING THE SUNDAY HOLY

We keep the Sunday holy by showing respect for the preaching and God's Word at the church services and by gladly hearing and learning the Word.

He entered, as His custom was, into the synagogue on the sabbath day (Luke 4:16).

I was glad when they said unto me, Let us go unto the house of the Lord (Ps. 122:1).

The word have I laid up in my heart, that I might not sin against Thee (Ps. 119:11).

Besides going to church, a Christian should so use the Sunday that he becomes spiritually and physically refreshed for his Monday morning work.

6. THE CHURCH YEAR

The purpose of the church year is an orderly meditation upon the principal events in the life of Christ and upon

His life and teaching. The church year begins with the First Sunday in Advent which comes in the last part of November or the first part of December. The church year is divided into two main parts. The festal part, from the beginning of Advent to Pentecost Sunday, includes Christmas, Easter, and Pentecost. The other part consists of from 23 to 27 Trinity Sundays, depending upon the date of Easter. This part begins with the first Sunday after Pentecost.

Prayer:

Our God and Father, we thank Thee for the Lord's day, the day of rest and gladness. Help us to use the day in accordance with Thy will so that each one of us may become a better, stronger, more helpful, and happier Christian. May the day be filled with Thy praise, O Christ. Bless, O God, our congregation and our pastor. Grant that the preaching of Thy Word may be in the power of the Spirit so that the Word may reach our hearts. Amen.

WORD STUDY

Undefiled: not corrupted, not soiled. Affliction: trouble, misery. Meditation: continued thought.

QUESTIONS
(To be answered in writing, except 1 and 2)

1. Look up and read in your Bible the Bible passages quoted in this chapter. Underscore them in your Bible.
2. Be ready to recite the material that is to be memorized.
3. What does the word Sabbath mean?
4. For what purpose did God give Israel the Sabbath?
5. Which day was the day of rest in the Old Testament?
6. Why is the Old Testament Sabbath called a shadow of the things to come?
7. Give the reasons why the Old Testament Sabbath ceased when the New Testament covenant was established.
8. How did Sunday become our day of public worship and rest?
9. State the purpose of the Christian Sunday.
10. What spiritual blessings does the Christian Sunday bring us?
11. What physical blessings does it bring us?
12. What social blessings?
13. What does the Third Commandment instruct us to do?
14. How do we keep Sunday holy?
15. Explain how we show respect for God's Word.
16. In what ways do people misuse Sunday?
17. What is the purpose of the church year?
18. How is the church year divided?
19. Applying this lesson to ourselves, is there anything for which we need to pray God to forgive us?

BIBLE STUDY

1. What was the character of the Old Testament Sabbath according to Ex. 23:12 and Lev. 23:3?

2. Read in your Bible the passages cited in footnote 2 of this lesson and point out why Saturday as the day of rest and worship is not binding in the New Testament any more than circumcision or the other institutions mentioned.

3. Read Acts 20:7; I Cor. 16:2; and Rev. 1:10, and point out (1) practices followed, and (2) duties performed on the first day of the week, and (3) state the name used for this day.

THE CHURCH YEAR

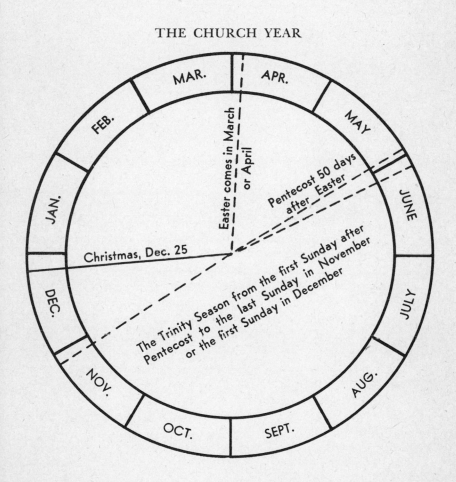

CHAPTER SIX

The Fourth Commandment

Honor thy father and thy mother, that thy days may be long upon the land which the Lord thy God giveth thee.

What does this mean?

Answer: We should fear and love God so that we do not despise our parents and superiors, nor provoke them to anger, but honor, serve, obey, love, and esteem them.

1. THE SECOND TABLE OF THE LAW

We come now to the second table of the law. The seven commandments of the second table teach love to our neighbor. Our neighbor is our fellow-man.

Thou shalt love thy neighbor as thyself (Matt. 22:39).

Only he who loves God can love his neighbor as himself. Love to our neighbor flows out of love to God.

2. MEMBER OF THREE INSTITUTIONS

A Christian is a member of three institutions, the family, the state, and the church. All three are of God.

The Fourth Commandment teaches how a Christian should live as a member of these institutions. There are things he should do and things he should not do.

Where people live together, each one has duties that must be fulfilled for his own sake as well as for the sake of the others. The Word of God expresses it this way:

Let each one of us please his neighbor for that which is good (Rom. 15:2).

22

3. THE FAMILY

A family consists of parents and children. Together they make a home.

I. Children. Children should not despise their parents nor provoke them to anger. Christian parents pray for their children, buy their food and clothing, protect them in danger, comfort them in sorrow, and watch over them in sickness. They share their joy and grief. They correct their mistakes and instruct them in the Word of God. There is not enough money in the world to pay for the sacrifices, love, and care of Christian parents. Children who despise such parents and provoke them to anger are thoughtless, selfish, and without gratitude.

There are parents whose sins make the home unhappy. In such homes the temptation for the children to despise the parents is often very great. Still, it would be sin to yield to the temptation. If the children pray for their parents and for themselves, God will help them to love and honor even a father and mother who fail in their duties.

Cursed be he that setteth light by his father or his mother (Deut. 27:16).

What then should the children do? They should honor, serve, obey, love, and esteem their parents. We honor a person when we serve, obey, love, and esteem him.

Children should protect the good name of their parents. By honoring their parents they honor God, their own home, and themselves.

An obedient child learns how to control himself, while a disobedient child yields to his desires and whims. The obedient child gladdens his parents and prepares himself for useful living. By lack of self-control the disobedient child stores up grief for himself and others.

Children, obey your parents in the Lord, for this is right. Honor thy father and mother, which is the first commandment with promise, that it may be well with thee, and thou mayest live long on the earth (Eph. 6:1-3).

II. Parents. To the parents God's Word says:

Ye fathers, provoke not your children to wrath, but nurture them in the chastening and admonition of the Lord (Eph. 6:4).

23

In order to train the children in Christian living, the parents themselves must live a Christian life. Parents who neglect these duties are sinning against God and their children.

Prayer for and with the children and family devotion are a necessary part of the training. It is equally necessary to teach the children obedience in order that they may learn self-control. When needed, punishments are used to teach the child to mind.

He that spareth his rod hateth his son, but he that loveth him chasteneth him betimes (Prov. 13:24).

The rod means anything that brings an unwilling child to obey, from a look and a word to the more severe punishments.

> O happy home, where Thou art loved the dearest,
> Thou loving Friend and Savior of our race,
> And where among the guests there never cometh
> One who can hold such high and honored place!
>
> O happy home, whose little ones are given
> To Thee, O Lord, in humble faith and prayer,
> To Thee, their Friend, who from the heights of heaven
> Guides them, and guards with more than mother's care!
>
> O happy home, where each one serves Thee lowly,
> Whatever his appointed work may be,
> Till ev'ry common task seems great and holy,
> When it is done, O Lord, as unto Thee!
>
> O happy home, where thou art not forgotten
> When joy is overflowing, full and free,
> O happy home, where ev'ry wounded spirit
> Is brought, Physician, Comforter, to Thee.
>
> (L. H. No. 537, vv. 1, 3, 4, 5)

4. THE STATE

The state is the large family, comprising all those who live in the land. It has a government, the duty of which is to govern in accordance with the laws of the land.

God's Word calls the government the higher powers and says that these powers are of God (Rom. 13:1). God has so planned this world that every state must have a government, otherwise there would be neither law nor order. It is for the people to decide what form of government they want.

The government should faithfully work for the welfare of the people according to the laws of the land. It is its duty to protect those who obey the laws and punish those who disobey. Every officer of the government should be honest and just, impartial and trustworthy. Of the ruler God's Word says:

He beareth not the sword in vain: for he is a minister of God (Rom. 13:4).

To the citizens God says:
Let every soul be in subjection to the higher powers (Rom. 13:1).

We are in subjection to the government (the higher powers) when we obey the laws of the country. A Christian should also pray for his country and its government and in his life and by his vote promote its welfare. This is true patriotism.

If the government should demand what the Word of God forbids, *we must obey God rather than men* (Acts 5:29).

Render unto Cæsar the things that are Cæsar's; and unto God the things that are God's (Matt. 22:21).

5. THE CHURCH

The church is the spiritual family to which the Christian belongs. It consists of all those who are baptized, believe in and obey Jesus Christ as their Savior and Lord. It is our spiritual home. (See Chapters Twenty-one and Twenty-two.)

It is the duty of a Christian to pray for the church, with its pastors, teachers, and all other workers; to be loyal to its teaching; and to support it to the best of his ability.

6. THE PROMISE

The promise added to the Fourth Commandment was especially given to Israel, but it is also a promise to other nations. A nation that honors father and mother because it fears and loves God, will obey His laws and walk righteously before God and men. Such a nation will be strong morally and physically. The individual shares in these blessings.

Prayer:

Dear heavenly Father, I thank Thee for father and mother, for home, country, and church. Help me to be more worthy of these blessings and forgive my sins against the Fourth Commandment. Teach me to honor father and mother, to become a good citizen and a true church member. O God, protect my parents, my home and all my dear ones, my church, and my country. May the government be just, and may the citizens be honest and true. In Jesus' name. Amen.

WORD STUDY

To set light by: to show contempt for. Chastening: disciplining, subduing. Admonition: advice, warning. Betimes: early, that is, early in life.

QUESTIONS
(To be answered in writing, except 1 and 2)

1. Look up and read in your Bible the Bible passages quoted in this chapter. Underscore them in your Bible.
2. Be ready to recite the material that is to be memorized.
3. Who is my neighbor?
4. What is our duty to our neighbor?
5. Name the three institutions to which a Christian belongs.
6. State some of the things good parents do for their children.
7. What would you say about children who despise such parents?
8. How should children act toward parents who are not good parents?
9. In what ways should children show gratitude to their parents?
10. Why is it necessary for children to learn to obey?
11. What is meant by "the rod"?
12. Name some of the duties of parents toward their children.
13. Why is family devotion important in the home?
14. What is the state?
15. State the duty of the government.
16. Why is a government necessary?
17. State the duties of the citizens toward the government.
18. Why should we obey God rather than men?
19. What is the church?
20. State the duties of the members toward the church.
21. How is the promise added to the Fourth Commandment fulfilled?

BIBLE STUDY

1. After reading I Sam. 2:12-17, state by what acts these priests transgressed against the Fourth Commandment.
2. How did Ruth honor her mother-in-law according to Ruth 1:14-18?
3. What example for children is given in Luke 2:51?
4. After reading II Thess. 1:11-12, state how this fits into what we have studied in this chapter.

26

CHAPTER SEVEN

The Fifth Commandment

Thou shalt not kill.

What does this mean?

Answer: We should fear and love God so that we do our neighbor no bodily harm nor cause him any suffering, but help and befriend him in every need.

1. VALUE OF HUMAN LIFE

Man's life has eternal value because he is created in the image of God. There are in every person untold possibilities for time and eternity. We are interested in life and love it. This love of life is created in us by God.

To God's children, life becomes even a much richer and more joyful experience. Their companionship with Christ makes it so. He understands, forgives, inspires, and strengthens and points forward to life eternal with Himself. Life thus becomes a glorious gift from God.

Security of life is one of our greatest necessities. Without such security we could neither enjoy what we have nor plan for the future.

In this commandment God has protected human life against wilful destruction. The first murderer was cursed (Gen. 4:11), and later God declared: *Whoso sheddeth man's blood, by man shall his blood be shed; for in the image of God made He man* (Gen. 9:6).

2. SIN AGAINST THE FIFTH COMMANDMENT

This commandment is transgressed in many ways.

There is the murderer who has shortened a person's day

of grace and destroyed an unfinished life. Lynching is mob murder. On our highways murder is committed almost every day by careless and reckless drivers. And then the millions of lives destroyed in unjust wars!

Neglecting to help others who are in bodily need is selfish cruelty and sin against the Fifth Commandment.

And let us not forget the murdering of souls, by enticing them to sin. Commercialized liquor traffic and vice, indecent movies, vicious magazine articles that destroy faith and morals, and the teaching that man is merely the highest animal and has no soul, are the world's ways of soul murder.

God's Word applies to all murderers in all ages:
"The voice of thy brother's blood crieth unto me from the ground. And now cursed art thou from the ground, which has opened its mouth to receive thy brother's blood from thy hand" (Gen. 4:10-11).

3. TAKING ONE'S OWN LIFE

He who destroys his own life is also a murderer.

If any man destroyeth the temple of God, him shall God destroy; for the temple of God is holy, and such are ye (that is, such temple are ye) (I Cor. 3:17).

God, the giver of life, is the only one who has the right to end it. It is both foolish and cowardly to run away from the consequences of our sins by resorting to suicide.

If we have sinned we should repent, for there is salvation in Jesus Christ even for the greatest sinner. Without Him remorse and despair will lead to acts that add sin to sin.

If we have heavy burdens to bear, let us remember that our Savior bore still heavier burdens for us. He often leads His friends through fire of trials to the highest spiritual life. He that trusts Him shall experience the truth of God's promise:

As thy days, so shall thy strength be (Deut. 33:25).

4. MOTIVES LEADING TO MURDER

Motives leading to murder are jealousy, hatred, desire for revenge, fear, and lust for money and power. In God's eyes the motives themselves are just as sinful as the act.

Whosoever hateth his brother is a murderer, and ye know that no murderer hath eternal life abiding in him (I John 3:15).

28

5. FULFILLING THE FIFTH COMMANDMENT

Fearing and loving God, we should help and befriend our neighbor in every bodily need.

In this world of sin there is suffering and need everywhere, even under the best conditions. The sick need care and the orphans need a home; the hungry need food and the weak need protection; the shut-ins need cheer and the fallen and wayward need to be rescued; the prisoners need help to begin life anew and all need God's saving and sanctifying love.

It is the privilege and responsibility of God's children to be His messengers of good-will and brotherly help to those in need. In this way we serve our Lord and Savior.

I was hungry, and ye gave Me to eat; I was thirsty, and ye gave Me drink; I was a stranger, and ye took Me in; naked and ye clothed Me; I was sick, and ye visited Me; I was in prison, and ye came unto Me.... Inasmuch as ye did it unto one of these My brethren, even these least, ye did it unto Me (Matt. 25:35-36 and 40).

6. LOVE YOUR ENEMIES

Christ goes even farther. He commands:

Love your enemies, do good to them that hate you, bless them that curse you, pray for them that despitefully use you (Luke 6:27-28).

7. SOCIAL DUTIES

But a Christian cannot stop even here. Business and politics are too often the instruments of injustice, and social conditions the agencies of vice. It becomes the Christian's privilege and duty to take an active interest in the civic affairs of his community and country. He must work that justice may prevail, security of life and home may be guaranteed, the opportunity to earn one's daily bread may exist, and the weak and unfortunate may be protected. Failure to exercise one's fullest influence for the good of others is sin.

To him that knoweth to do good, and doeth it not, to him it is sin (James 4:17).

Dear young friends, again we have seen what a Christian life should be. We also realize anew how much we need God's forgiveness for neglecting to serve Christ by neglecting to serve our neighbor; and we pray:

We thank Thee, our heavenly Father, that in Baptism we became Thy children and were given the privilege of being Thy messengers of good-will and Christian love to our neighbors. We are ashamed that we have done so badly, and humbly ask Thy forgiveness. Help us to love Thee better, that we may serve our neighbor in a warmer and truer Christian spirit. Strengthen all who are in sorrow and are bearing heavy burdens. Through their burdens may they be led closer to Thee, that they may experience that Thou givest the weary strength. We pray in Christ Jesus. Amen.

WORD STUDY

Remorse: hopeless anguish or grief. Despitefully: in an insulting way. Social: what pertains to the human society, the human family.

QUESTIONS

(To be answered in writing, except 1 and 2)

1. Look up and read in your Bible the Bible passages quoted in this chapter. Underscore them in your Bible.
2. Be ready to recite the material that is to be memorized.
3. Why is human life more valuable than the life of animals?
4. How did man acquire his love of life?
5. What makes life a more glorious gift to God's children than to others?
6. Why is security of life one of our greatest needs?
7. List different ways in which murder is committed.
8. What does God say about murderers?
9. How do men sin against the Fifth Commandment without committing actual murder?
10. What does God's Word say about him who destroys his own life?
11. How can we be saved from despair when the burdens of life become very heavy?
12. State motives leading to murder.
13. What does God say about evil motives?
14. What are we to do to our neighbor according to the Fifth Commandment?
15. State some of the bodily needs found everywhere.
16. State what Christ said of those who had helped His brethren in bodily need.
17. Whom did He call His brethren?
18. Make a list of the civic duties of a Christian.
19. How should a Christian use his vote?
20. State what God's Word says of those who neglect to use an opportunity to do good.
21. What is the practical value of this commandment?

BIBLE STUDY

1. Read Ex. 1:22; Gen. 37:18-28; I Kings 21:11-16; and Luke 10: 25-37; and tell how these different persons sinned against the Fifth Commandment.
2. After reading I Sam. 24:16-18; Matt. 27:3-5; and Mark 14:66-72; explain why these men acted differently in the dark hour of their lives.

30

CHAPTER EIGHT

The Sixth Commandment

Thou shalt not commit adultery.

What does this mean?

Answer: We should fear and love God so that we lead a chaste and pure life in word and deed, and that husband and wife love and honor each other.

1. MARRIAGE GOD'S INSTITUTION

God created man and woman to be a help for each other and He joined them in marriage.[1]

"And Jehovah God said, It is not good that the man should be alone; I will make him a help meet for him. . . . And the rib, which Jehovah God had taken from the man, made He a woman, and brought her unto the man" (Gen. 2:18 and 22).

And God blessed them (Gen. 1:28).

Marriage, as every other gift from God, is always in danger of being destroyed by sin. For its protection God has given the Sixth Commandment: Thou shalt not commit adultery. The danger comes from the abuse of the sex forces. Given by God, these forces must be controlled by God if they shall serve His purpose.

---

[1] Originally each man had only one wife. This is called monogamy. Polygamy (that a man has several wives) came as a result of the falling away from God. The practice started among the descendants of Cain (Gen. 4:23). While Noah and his sons each had only one wife, polygamy little by little crept in again, and at the time of Abraham it had become an established practice recognized by law everywhere. Though God tolerated polygamy in Israel, the laws and institutions He gave aimed at restoring the original form of marriage. At the time of Jesus, monogamy had been established among the Jews.

Let us together in Jesus' name study this great problem in our life.

2. HOME BUILDING

Marriage leads to home building. Young people naturally dream of a home of their own filled with love and happiness. If they think and not only dream, they want to prepare themselves for building a happy home. It is a serious task and it takes more than the wedding ceremony to make one a home builder.

There are especially three things we should consider.

I. Only clean people can build happy homes. One reason is that God cannot live in an impure heart and without God the home builders are doomed to bitter disappointments.

Blessed are the pure in heart, for they shall see God (Matt. 5:8).

There is another reason why only clean people can build happy homes. Only a clean mind loves clean thoughts and only he whose mind is clean, will speak and act in a clean spirit. Being filthy inside, a person cannot help but be filthy in his life. Impurity is an awful master. Having gained control of the mind, impurity holds it in an iron grip.

II. Then we have the second consideration. We must be ready to meet the duties of family life, the man as bread winner and father and the woman as homemaker and mother. Failure to work and sacrifice for the welfare of home and children has ruined many a marriage.

III. The third consideration has to do with the choosing of the life mate. Do not act thoughtlessly and on the spur of a sudden emotion. Use Christian common sense and look for common sense in the one you choose. The two should agree on the religious life of the home and to what church they should belong. They should come to an understanding on such matters as the kind of home life they aim at, the bringing up of the children God may give them, the finances of the home, and the amusements in which they will take part. A family divided on such questions is headed for much trouble.

In choosing a mate, a Christian will speak to God and seek His will and also listen to the advice of parents.

Let marriage be had in honor among all (Heb. 13:4).

3. CLEAN MIND AND BODY

We must learn to control our thought life and our sex forces. For the sin begins in the heart.

I say unto you, that every one that looketh on a woman to lust after her hath committed adultery with her already in his heart (Matt. 5:28).

However, true love between man and woman is not impure. There is a world of difference between lust and love. Lust is selfish, seeks only its own satisfaction and is therefore degrading. Love is unselfish, seeks the welfare and happiness of the other person and is therefore uplifting.

How can we keep clean in mind and body? A mind that is not occupied with worth while things becomes a playground for evil lusts and desires. Take interest in your work, your church, the affairs of your community and country. Cultivate interest in good reading, in song and music, and in clean fun. Choose as your friends boys and girls who have such interests. Be a missionary for Christian living among the young people. Have a purpose in life.

Shun like poison indecent or even questionable pictures, movies, and magazines. Keep away from people who talk about little else than sex. Do not submit to fashions in dress that specialize in sex appeal. Flee from them. Joseph found it safest to flee from the temptation. It is more manly to flee from the devil than to be overcome by him.

You say that this is not easy to do. Of course it is not. Still, there is one who not only will make such a life possible, but who will make you determined to live no other life. It is Jesus Christ. Submit your life to His control, live close to Him in His Word and in prayer, watch so that the tempter does not trap you unawares, and hold fast to the forgiveness of your sins. You will then experience a freedom, a strength, and a joy found nowhere else.

Watch and pray, that ye enter not into temptation (Matt. 26:41).

Apart from Me ye can do nothing (John 15:5).

4. HUSBAND AND WIFE

Husband and wife should love and honor one another.

A home is not built by what we purchase at the stores. It is the love and respect husband and wife have for each other and their consideration, faithfulness, and courage that make a home. The poorest house where a family lives in mutual love and respect becomes "home, sweet home." The finest mansion where the members of the family are separated by selfishness, jealousy, and strife is nothing but a lodging, a place where one eats and sleeps and keeps one's belongings.

5. DIVORCE

About divorce Christ says:

I say unto you, that everyone that putteth away his wife, saving for the cause of fornication, maketh her an adulteress, and whosoever shall marry her when she is put away committeth adultery (Matt. 5:32).

What therefore God hath joined together, let not man put asunder (Matt. 19:6).

The law of the state may permit divorce for various causes, but all who fear and love God are subject to the higher law, the Word of God. According to the Word of God marriage is for life. We do not grow into Christian manhood by running away from our difficulties.

The children are the greatest sufferers when the home is broken up. If the parents remarry, the children are seldom welcome in the home of either parent. They have lost both father and mother.

6. THE UNMARRIED

There are many who for one reason or another never marry. Among them are men and women who are the salt of the earth. Many homes lean heavily on some unmarried uncle or aunt or on an unmarried child. God bless them.

Prayer:

We thank Thee, Father in heaven, that we also here on earth have homes where we may live a family life in love and happiness. Keep us close to our Lord Jesus Christ that we like Him may be pure and clean in thoughts and deeds in order that our conduct may be to Thy honor. Then it will be to our true welfare. Amen.

WORD STUDY

Adultery: When a married person has sex relations with one to whom he is not married. Fornication: adultery. Lust: impure desire.

34

QUESTIONS
(To be answered in writing, except 1 and 2)

1. Look up and read in your Bible the Bible passages quoted in this chapter. Underscore them in your Bible.
2. Be ready to recite the material that is to be memorized.
3. Why did God institute marriage?
4. Why did God protect marriage by giving the Sixth Commandment?
5. What danger may be caused by the sex forces?
6. Give the reason why young people should prepare themselves for home building.
7. State how a young person should prepare himself for this task.
8. Why should we learn to control our thought life?
9. State the difference between lust and love.
10. If we are to keep clean in mind and body we must be interested in what is good for ourselves and others. Why?
11. Enumerate things in which we should be interested.
12. Why can we not play with what is indecent and questionable and still keep clean in our mind?
13. Give a list of things to be shunned.
14. Why do we need Christ if we shall succeed in keeping clean in mind and body?
15. What then must be our relation to Him?
16. Explain the freedom, strength, and joy that Christ gives.
17. State what the love and honor of husband and wife for each other have to do with the happiness of the home.
18. List the marks of a Christian home.
19. Give the reason why marriage is for life
20. Why are the children the greatest sufferers in cases of divorce?
21. In what ways has this chapter given you help and inspiration for your own life?

BIBLE STUDY

1. Read Gen. 39:7-12 and describe the character of the two persons involved.
2. After reading I Cor. 9:26-27, point out (1) what Paul's aim was; (2) what dangers threatened him; and (3) what means he used to counteract these dangers

CHAPTER NINE

The Seventh Commandment

Thou shalt not steal.

What does this mean?

Answer: We should fear and love God so that we do not rob our neighbor of his money or property, nor bring them into our possession by unfair dealing or fraud, but help him to improve and protect his property and living.

1. PROPERTY

A person's property consists of all material things that he rightfully owns. Money is used as a medium of exchange for service and goods.

We all need property such as food, clothing, shelter, and the means necessary for making our living.

2. GOD THE OWNER

God is the owner of all things.

The earth is the Lord's, and the fulness thereof (I Cor. 10:26)

The silver is Mine, and the gold is Mine, saith the Lord of hosts (Hag. 2:8)

The earth and its riches were here before we came and will be here when we are gone. These riches of field and forest and mine and sea and air are so abundant that there is more than enough for the material welfare of all people if used according to God's will.

36

3. MAN A STEWARD

God made man His steward of all these riches.

And God said unto them, Be fruitful, and multiply, and replenish the earth, and subdue it; and have dominion over the fish of the sea, and over the birds of the heavens, and over every living thing that moveth upon the earth (Gen. 1:28).

As stewards we are under a double responsibility. We should acquire property as well as use it according to our heavenly Father's will

4. ACQUIRING PROPERTY

God wants us to acquire property through work. Man was created to work. Adam and Eve had work to do even before the fall (Gen. 2:15). Our homes rest on work and on the safe possession of what we have honestly acquired. It is work that makes progress and civilization possible. Laziness is sin and causes want and suffering.

If any will not work, neither let him eat (II Thess. 3:10).

The sinfulness of the human heart has devised many means for getting property and money without work. Stealing, robbing, cheating, and using false weights and measures are practiced by some. Underpaying workers, "loafing on the job," catering to people's weakness and passions in order to sell wares that are harmful (the liquor traffic and the like), and gambling are other ways in which this commandment is broken. God's condemnation is upon all such.

Neither thieves, nor covetous . . . nor extortioners shall inherit the kingdom of God (I Cor. 6:10).

A young man lay on his deathbed. One day he asked his brother to go to a certain photographer and tell him that the young man several years ago had taken 3-4 inexpensive pictures from a pile on the table in the studio. The brother was to pay for the pictures and ask forgiveness for the theft. When he came back with the message of forgiveness, the young man said: "It was a small thing, but I had to get it off my conscience. I know that God also forgives. Now I can die in peace."

"We should fear and love God so that we do not rob our neighbor of his money and property nor bring them into

our possession by unfair dealing or fraud," as the Catechism says.

5. USING PROPERTY

Even though we have gained our property honestly we are not at liberty to use it as we may please. Possession of property, however little, involves responsibility. We should so use our property that we promote our own as well as our neighbor's material and spiritual welfare. Surrounding ourselves with luxury and selfish pleasure or using our property to satisfy vanity and pride is sin.

It is required in stewards, that a man be found faithful (I Cor. 4:2).

6. HELPING OUR NEIGHBOR

We help our neighbor to improve his property and living: 1. by dealing fairly and honestly with him in Christian love, and 2. by working for such social conditions as will make it possible for an honest man to earn a decent living and to keep his property.

A society of thieves cannot prosper, nor can a society controlled by brutal selfishness. The weak and unfortunate must be protected and helped and the fear and love of God should govern us in all financial affairs.

"We should fear and love God so that we . . . help our neighbor to improve and protect his property and living," to repeat the Catechism.

7. GIVING

God's many gifts and blessings make a Christian thankful. Gratitude, in order to live and grow, must express itself in thank-offerings and gifts. The thank-offerings in Israel were means used in developing the gratitude we meet in many of the Psalms (See such Psalms as 100; 136; 145 to 150). These thank-offerings were either regulated by law (mainly the tithe[1]) or were free-will offerings. The thank-offerings in the New Testament are all free-will offerings.

---

[1]The tithe (one tenth of the income) in the Old Testament constituted the principal tax for the support of the government, the church, and the poor, according to the Mosaic Law.

The other taxes demanded by the law were the temple tax, a kind of head tax paid once a lifetime, and the firstfruit. Both were very small. Later the kings imposed other taxes not known to the law.

38

Such offerings we should give gladly, freely, regularly, and as God prospers us.

God loveth a cheerful giver (II Cor. 9:7).

Upon the first day of the week let each one of you lay by him in store, as he may prosper (I Cor. 16:2).

8. BUILDING CHARACTER

The use of property and money according to God's will builds Christian character. A man develops honesty when dealing fairly with others in money matters. He develops dishonesty by unfair dealings.

We build both honesty and dependability when paying our debts. He that does not exert himself in paying his just debt, becomes careless, dishonest, and unreliable.

The wicked borroweth and payeth not again (Ps. 37:21).

Debt is easily acquired, but hard to pay. God's Word admonishes us to keep out of debt

Owe no man anything, save to love one another (Rom. 13:8).

We develop unselfishness and liberality by giving gladly to those who are in need.

When handling money and property according to God's will, we also learn to be economical and saving. Contrary to widespread belief, selfish spending brings no happiness. To squander and waste like the Prodigal Son is sin. When Jesus had made a boy's lunch serve as a full meal for five thousand people, He told His disciples:

Gather up the broken pieces ... that nothing be lost (John 6:12).

If we give gladly, freely, and as God prospers us, saving will not make us greedy misers. It is only by being thrifty that most of us are able to give freely and gladly.

Prayer:

We thank Thee, our heavenly Father, that Thou hast made us stewards over the riches of the earth. Forgive us that we so often have been selfish and unfaithful stewards, and help us so to fear and love Thee that we may deal honestly and in brotherly love with all people. Amen.

WORD STUDY

Steward: as used in this chapter a steward is a manager of another person's property. Covetous: those who covet (see Ninth and Tenth Commandments). Extortioner: one who uses force, torture, threat, or other illegal means to take away other people's property.

QUESTIONS
(To be answered in writing, except 1 and 2)

1. Look up and read in your Bible the Bible passages quoted in this chapter. Underscore them in your Bible.
2. Be ready to recite the material that is to be memorized.
3. What is property?
4. Why do we all need property?
5. State why God is the owner of all things.
6. When did God make man steward of His riches?
7. What are our responsibilities as stewards?
8. Describe the right way of acquiring property.
9. And the wrong way.
10. Describe the wrong way of using property.
11. How should we use it?
12. In what ways can we help our neighbor to improve his property and living?
13. What should be our motive in giving?
14. State the New Testament rule for giving.
15. How does the use of property and money help in building Christian character?
16. What does God's Word say of him who borrows and does not pay his debt?
17. Why should we be thrifty?
18. Describe how a thrifty Christian may escape becoming a miser.
19. State as many reasons for poverty as you can think of.
20. And for people becoming well-to-do
21. What do you think of the prayer we read in Prov. 30:8, the last half of the verse?

BIBLE STUDY

After reading II Cor. 8:1-5, point out (1) the financial circumstances of the Macedonians, (2) the spirit in which they gave, and (3) the extent of their giving.

The Eighth Commandment

Thou shalt not bear false witness against thy neighbor.

What does this mean?

Answer: We should fear and love God so that we do not deceitfully belie, betray, backbite; nor slander our neighbor, but apologize for him, speak well of him, and put the most charitable construction on all that he does.

1. A GOOD NAME

A good name is part of our daily bread.

Everyday experiences tell us that people are unwilling to employ a person who has the reputation of being dishonest and unreliable. On the other hand, many are chosen for positions of trust and responsibility purely on their reputation for honesty and dependability.

Truly, a good reputation belongs to our daily bread.

A good name is rather to be chosen than great riches (Prov. 22:1)

2. FALSE WITNESSING

This is what God forbids. We bear false witness against our neighbor when we belie, betray, backbite, and slander him. Sometimes we damage our neighbor's good name by the spirit and tone in which we say what otherwise might be harmless. Helping to create a wrong impression about our neighbor is sin against the Eighth Commandment. It is extremely humiliating when even Christians do some of these things.

People bear false witness against their neighbors either because they hope to gain something for themselves by hurting others, or because they have a grudge against them and want revenge, or simply because they love to spread gossip and rumors.

There is a great deal of hypocrisy in all slander and back-biting. Covering up our evil intention when slandering our neighbor, we pretend to be above all the wicked things of which he is guilty. But God knows how false our pretensions are.

Putting away falsehood, speak ye truth each one with his neighbor, for we are members one of another (Eph. 4:25).

Lie not one to another (Col. 3:9).

3. THE FATHER OF LIES

The devil was the first false witness. Slyly he induced Eve (and Adam) to believe that God had not told the full truth when He said that they should die the day they ate of the tree of knowledge.

Let us recall what Jesus said of the devil:

He was a murderer from the beginning, and standeth not in the truth, because there is no truth in him. When he speaketh a lie, he speaketh of his own, for he is a liar, and the father thereof (John 8:44).

Being the father of lies, the devil tempts us to bear false witness against our neighbor.

The devil having already put into the heart of Judas Iscariot, Simon's son, to betray Jesus (John 13:2).

It is the devil's work we do when we bear false witness against our neighbor!

4. COURT CASES

Not only the welfare of individuals, but even the welfare of society is at stake in court cases. Lying witnesses, dishonest lawyers and juries, and judges who let the guilty go free because of sentimentality, political "pull" or bribes, sin against God, the individual, and society; and society by no means suffers the least. Respect for law and order is destroyed, lawlessness is encouraged, and security and orderly progress are endangered.

He that justifieth the wicked, and he that condemneth the righteous, both of them alike are an abomination to the Lord (Prov. 17:15).

5. OUR REPUTATION PROTECTED

A good name is so valuable that God used one of the Ten Commandments to safeguard it. We should apologize for our neighbor, speak well of him, and put the most charitable construction on all that he does.

How should this be done in daily practice? Examples from the life of Christ will help us. One day the disciples came upon a man who drove out demons in the name of Christ and they forbade him to do it because he, did not follow them. When Jesus heard it, He told them not to forbid him and added that the man's work proved that he was not against Christ but for Him (Mark 9:38-39). When crucified, Christ even put a charitable construction on this vile, bloodthirsty act of His enemies. He said:

Father, forgive them; for they know not what they do (Luke 23:34).

If this spirit of Christ is in us, we too will protect the good name of our neighbor.

6. SPEAKING TRUTH IN LOVE

The apostle instructs us that we, "speaking truth in love, may grow up in all things into Him, who is the head, even Christ" (Eph. 4:15).

If we are to speak truth in love we must have respect for truth, and we must love our neighbor. Such respect and love are not the product of the mind but an attitude of the heart. It requires a molding of the heart which only the Holy Spirit can do when we trust, obey, and follow Christ.

Face to face with Him, who never tampered with the truth and never offended against love, we all realize that we are only beginners in the keeping of the Eighth Commandment.

Prayer:

Lord Jesus Christ, bear with our sinfulness and the many uncharitable words that pass our lips. Make us sorry and forgive us. Help us to live in fellowship with Thee that we, too, may learn of Thee to speak the truth in love. Protect our neighbor from evil and bless him in body and soul for Thine own sake. Amen.

WORD STUDY

Backbite: speak evil of one in his absence. Apologize: offer excuse for what seems to be a fault of another. Belie: tell an untruth. Betray: to deal treacherously, "sell out" another, "double-cross." Slander: circulate false statements. Hypocrisy: duplicity.

QUESTIONS
(To be answered in writing, except 1 and 2)

1. Look up and read in your Bible the Bible passages quoted in this chapter. Underscore them in your Bible.
2. Be ready to recite the material that is to be memorized.
3. What is meant by a good reputation?
4. Why does God in this commandment protect our reputation?
5. State different ways in which men bear false witness against their neighbors.
6. What are the motives that prompt us to bear false witness?
7. Give the reason why one who bears false witness is a hypocrite.
8. Why did Jesus call the devil "the father of lies"?
9. How did the devil lie to Adam and Eve?
10. Who moved Judas to betray Jesus?
11. Whom do all false witnesses serve?
12. Who sins against this commandment in court cases?
13. Who suffers from such acts?
14. To speak truth in love is not a product of the mind but an attitude of the heart. Why?
15. How may we learn to speak truth in love?
16. Why did Jesus never tell a "white lie"?

BIBLE STUDY

1. After reading Acts 6:7-14 and Acts 7:54-60, point out (a) what religious and national interests motivated the enemies of Stephen (verses 7 and 14) ; (b) what other emotions undoubtedly influenced them (verse 10) ; (c) the kind of witnesses they used; (d) how they silenced the testimony of Stephen; (e) Stephen's attitude.
2. In the light of the Eighth Commandment, what must be said of the motives and actions of these people?
3. What does God's Word say about doing evil in the defense of a good cause? (See Rom. 3:8 and 6:1.)

44

CHAPTER ELEVEN

The Ninth and Tenth Commandments

THE NINTH COMMANDMENT

Thou shalt not covet thy neighbor's house.

What does this mean?

Answer: We should fear and love God so that we do not seek by craftiness to gain possession of our neighbor's inheritance or home, nor obtain them under pretense of a legal right, but assist and serve him in keeping the same.

THE TENTH COMMANDMENT

Thou shalt not covet thy neighbor's wife, nor his man-servant, nor his maid-servant, nor his cattle, nor anything that is thy neighbor's.

What does this mean?

Answer: We should fear and love God so that we do not estrange or entice away our neighbor's wife, servants, or cattle, but seek to have them remain and discharge their duty to him.

These two commandments deal with coveting and may therefore be studied together. There is a difference, though, in that the Ninth Commandment speaks of a man's real estate and the Tenth of his personal property. In the days of Moses even a man's wife was considered his property.

1. COVETING

The word covet as used in these commandments means to be filled with an evil desire or lust for that which belongs to another. It is the fertile soil out of which sinful actions grow.

Coveting is sin and makes a man miserable. He desires something he cannot have because it belongs to his neighbor. If he does not work to overcome the temptation by confessing it to God and pleading His forgiveness and help, the desire will torture him into planning and scheming how he may obtain what his lust craves. He will resort to underhanded means, even to such crimes as murder. Coveting has ruined the man's own life as well as the life of his neighbor.

Take heed, and keep yourselves from all covetousness (Luke 12:15).

2. COVETOUSNESS AND PROGRESS

We should notice the difference between coveting and the longing for improvement and progress. Coveting desires what belongs to someone else and uses un-Christian means to gain possession of it. The wish to improve one's living is concerned with one's progress through Christian means, such as work, study, industriousness, and thrift. It goes hand in hand with assisting and serving our neighbor in keeping his inheritance and home.

THE CONCLUSION

What does God declare concerning all the Commandments?

I the Lord thy God am a jealous God, visiting the iniquity of the fathers upon the children unto the third and fourth generation of them that hate Me; and showing mercy unto thousands of them that love Me and keep My commandments (Ex. 20:5).

What does this mean?

Answer: God threatens to punish all who transgress these commandments. We should, therefore, fear His wrath, and in no wise break them. But He promises grace and every blessing to all who keep them. We should, therefore, love Him, trust Him, and gladly keep His commandments.

46

3. GOD'S PUNISHMENT

Unpunished sin would be a double curse. It would lead man deeper and deeper into wickedness and it would keep him from heeding God's call to repentance. It is the penalty, the consequences of sin, that makes man stop and think.

There is a fearful seriousness in what God says of the punishment of sin.

The soul that sinneth, it shall die (Ez. 18:4).

Be not deceived; God is not mocked; for whatsoever a man soweth, that shall he also reap. For he that soweth unto his own flesh shall of the flesh reap corruption (Gal. 6:7-8).

The manner of the punishment is manifold. The agony of an accusing conscience is one form. Loss of honor, health, friends, and property are other forms. Eternal separation from God, which Jesus calls the judgment of hell (Matt. 23:33), is the last and worst punishment.

Even the sins of the fathers come as punishment upon children who hate God. The evil reputation of the parents, the results of immorality, of drunkenness, and of other forms of ungodliness are inherited and increased in children who continue in the same evil ways. Thus sin becomes a destructive curse from generation to generation. And individuals, families, and society suffer.

4. GOD'S BLESSING

God shows mercy to man in order to encourage, inspire, and enable him to live according to God's will. Mercy is kindness and compassion to the condemned. It is not only undeserved, but the very opposite of what we have deserved.

In the first place, God blots out even the worst sins of the repenting sinner through forgiveness for Christ's sake. He gives peace in a good conscience. He keeps and guards us from sin and its evil fruits in soul and body, and He makes us a blessing to other people. It is, of course, impossible in this life to be freed from all the bitter results of one's own sins or of the sins of parents. Still, God uses even these sufferings as a means for the building up of the spiritual life and Christian personality in His children. The fear and love of God are the strongest building forces in human life, while sin is the greatest destroyer.

47

We know that to them that love God all things work together for good (Rom. 8:28).

The blessings do not stop with the individual, but are in many ways inherited by the children and shared by society. The human family is so closely knit together that we transmit to our children both the fruits of our sins and the blessings of a God-fearing life.

The lovingkindness of Jehovah is from everlasting to everlasting upon them that fear Him, and His righteousness unto children's children (Ps. 103:17).

Godliness is profitable for all things, having promise of the life which now is, and of that which is to come (I Tim. 4:8).

* * *

In our studies of the commandments we have learned how our heavenly Father wants His children to live. It is a beautiful life, pure, strong, victorious, and governed by love to God and to our neighbor.

We have also come to realize that the best of us are far from perfect. We have done many things God has forbidden. In addition, we lack the purity of motives, the wholeheartedness and fulness of love that both God and His children look for. Even our hearts are corrupt and filled with evil lust.

This is the first lesson in the study of God's way of salvation. We are all lost sinners and need forgiveness of sin.

This forgiveness God provided by sending His Son to die for us and by giving us His Holy Spirit who enables us to believe in Jesus Christ unto salvation.

Of this Triune God and His salvation in Christ Jesus, the Catechism teaches in the second main part which contains the Three Articles of Faith.

Prayer:

Our heavenly Father, we thank Thee most sincerely for what Thou hast taught us in the commandments. We praise Thee for the beauty, joy, and inspiration experienced by Thy children when they live in loving obedience to Thee. We confess that our obedience is very imperfect and that only through Thy forgiveness of our sins can we continue to be Thy children and grow in Christ-likeness. Give us Thy Holy Spirit that we may fear and love Thee ever more in Christ Jesus. Amen.

WORD STUDY

Craftiness: the use of cunning, deceit; trickery. Pretense of a legal right: using the law to obtain property to which one has no just claim. Entice: lure, coax, charm (like a snake charmer). Jealous: used of God, it means that He will not permit sin to destroy His plan to save man; therefore, He punishes sin. Iniquity: wickedness. Grace: the free, unmerited favor and love of God. Flesh: sinful human nature.

QUESTIONS

(To be answered in writing, except 1 and 2)

1. Look up and read in your Bible the Bible passages quoted in this chapter. Underscore them in your Bible.
2. Be ready to recite the material that is to be memorized.
3. What is the meaning of the word "covet"?
4. State the meaning of (1) craftiness; (2) obtain under pretense of legal right.
5. Why does coveting make a man miserable?
6. How can coveting be overcome?
7. Point out the difference between coveting and the longing for improvement and progress.
8. Explain the meaning of (1) jealous, used of God; (2) iniquity; (3) grace.
9. Why would unpunished sin be a curse?
10. How does God punish sin?
11. In what ways do the sins of the fathers become a punishment upon children who hate God?
12. State the meaning of "mercy."
13. How does God show His mercy in regard to our sins?
14. Explain why the fear and love of God are strong building forces in human life.
15. Why is sin a destroyer in human life?
16. Who alone can keep God's commandments gladly?
17. Describe the kind of life God wants His children to lead, and state (1) whether this is a happy life, and (2) if so, why?
18. Why is it that even the best of us are sinners before God?
19. State the first lesson in the study of God's way of salvation.
20. How has God provided salvation for lost and condemned sinners?
21. Where in the Catechism do we learn of the Savior God has sent?

BIBLE STUDY

Read Psalm 1 and point out (1) the contrast between the man that is blessed and the wicked; (2) why the blessed is likened to a tree planted by the streams of water; (3) by what streams of water he is planted; (4) how he likes these streams of water (see v. 2); (5) how it helps the righteous that God knows his way (compare John 10:14 and 27-29); (6) why the wicked is likened to chaff; (7) what will be his judgment.

CHAPTER TWELVE

The Creed

The second main part of the Catechism consists of the Three Articles of Faith. These articles are also called the Apostolic Creed.

A creed is a statement of what one believes. The three articles set forth what the Christian Church believes and teaches about God. They came into existence in the earliest days of the church and have since been confessed by the millions of Christians throughout the centuries.

In these articles each one confesses his personal faith. The articles begin, "I believe." It is you, the reader, who says, "I believe." God grant that each one of us may truthfully make this glorious confession.

I. ONE GOD IN THREE PERSONS

In these articles of faith I confess that I believe in God the Father, the Son, and the Holy Spirit, that is, in the Triune God. The word triune means three in one. God is one God in three persons.

To us there is one God, the Father, of whom are all things, and we unto Him (I Cor. 8:6).

It is in the New Testament God has revealed that He is Father, Son, and Holy Spirit. When Jesus was baptized, the Father spoke from heaven, the Son was baptized, and the Spirit came upon Him (Matt. 3:16-17). Jesus spoke of the three persons as equals when He said,

*Make disciples of all the nations, baptizing them into the
name of the Father and of the Son and of the Holy Spirit*
(Matt. 28:19) . See also II Cor. 13:14.

The work of all three persons is necessary to my salvation. This I believe because it is the teaching of the Bible,
not because I understand it. God would be too small a God
for me if I could understand His mysteries. He would even
be smaller than I am, for I cannot explain the mystery that
I consist of body, soul, and spirit, and still I am one person.

THE FIRST ARTICLE—OF CREATION

*I believe in God the Father Almighty, Maker of heaven
and earth.*

What does this mean?

*Answer: I believe that God has created me and all that exists;
that He has given and still preserves to me my body and soul, my
eyes and ears, and all my members, my reason and all the powers
of my soul, together with food and raiment, home and family, and
all my property;*

*that He daily provides abundantly for all the needs of my life,
protects me from all danger, and guards and keeps me from all evil;*

*and that He does this purely out of fatherly and divine goodness
and mercy, without any merit or worthiness in me;*

*for all which I am in duty bound to thank, praise, serve and
obey Him. This is most certainly true.*

2. GOD

The Bible takes God for granted. We do not seek God
because we can prove that there is a God. We seek Him because we need Him. Our first need is to learn to know Him.

God has made Himself known through the world He
created and through His Word

*The heavens declare the glory of God; and the firmament
showeth His handiwork* (Ps. 19:1) .

As a building speaks of a builder, so nature speaks of
God, the almighty and wise creator.

> The starry heavens Thy rule obey,
> The earth maintains her place,
> And these Thy servants, night and day,
> Thy skill and power express.
>
> (L. H., No. 573, v. 3)

Still, in nature, we do not find the God who saves sinners
for nature tells nothing about Jesus Christ. Him we learn to
know in God's Word.

51

3. GOD THE FATHER

In this article I confess that I believe in God the Father. God is the Father of Jesus Christ and of all who are baptized into Christ and believe on Him as their Lord and Savior. So even I may call Him Father.

4. OTHER FACTS ABOUT GOD

God has revealed that He is spirit, and that He is eternal, everywhere present, all knowing, wise, almighty, and holy. These are called His attributes. These attributes belong to all three persons in the godhead. The Son and the Holy Spirit are as eternal, almighty, and holy as the Father.

God is a Spirit (John 4:24).

Being Spirit, God has no beginning and no end. He is eternal.

Before the mountains were brought forth or ever Thou hadst formed the earth and the world, even from everlasting to everlasting Thou art God (Ps. 90:2).

Being Spirit, God is not limited by any body or form. He is everywhere. This we call God's omnipresence.

Do not I fill heaven and earth, saith the Lord (Jer. 23:24).

God also sees, hears, and knows all things. He is omniscient.

God . . . knoweth all things (I John 3:20).

Under all circumstances He finds the right means for doing the right thing. He never makes a mistake. God is wise.

The Lord is wonderful in counsel and excellent in wisdom (Is. 28:29).

God is able to do whatever in His wisdom and goodness He decides. He is almighty.

Whatsoever the Lord pleased, that hath He done, in heaven and in earth, in the seas and in all deeps (Ps. 135:6).

There is no imperfection, injustice, or uncleanness in God. He is holy.

Holy, holy, holy is the Lord of hosts; the whole earth is full of His glory (Is. 6:3).

Such is our heavenly Father. And in all His work He is moved by love.

God is love (I John 4:8).

It is this Father that has created me and all that exists.

5. GOD USES HUMAN LANGUAGE

When the Bible speaks of God's eyes, ears, mouth, hands, and feet, it simply means that God sees, hears, speaks, acts, and moves. He is a living person.

In revealing Himself, God must use the language man understands.

> My God, how wonderful Thou art,
> Thou everlasting Friend!
> On Thee I stay my trusting heart
> Till faith in vision end.
> (L. H., No. 64, v. 7)

Prayer:

Heavenly Father, I marvel at Thy majesty, wisdom, power, holiness, and love. Truly Thou art God and there is none beside Thee. I rejoice that Thou didst baptize me unto sonship and art now my Father in Christ. Glory, honor, and praise be unto Thee for ever and ever. Amen.

WORD STUDY

Attributes: characteristics, qualities.

QUESTIONS

(To be answered in writing, except 1 and 2)

1. Look up and read in your Bible the Bible passages quoted in this chapter. Underscore them in your Bible.
2. Be ready to recite the material that is to be memorized.
3. Why do we call the three Articles of Faith "The Creed"?
4. About how old are these articles?
5. Why do the articles begin "I believe"?
6. State the meaning of triune.
7. Give the reason why you believe that God is triune.
8. Through what means has God revealed Himself?
9. Why cannot nature teach us the way of salvation?
10. Where is the way of salvation made known to us?
11. State what we mean when speaking of God's attributes.
12. Explain the meaning of each of the following attributes: eternal, omnipresent, omniscient, wise, almighty, holy.
13. Why did God use human language when making Himself known to men?
14. State (1) how God became your Father, and (2) what it means to you that He is your Father.

BIBLE STUDY

1. Read Ps. 19:1-6 and point out how the heavens declare the glory of God.
2. Read Ps. 136 and point out how God revealed Himself in the history of Israel.
3. How many times does Jesus use the word Father in John 14? Of whom does He use it?

53

CHAPTER THIRTEEN

The First Article --

GOD THE CREATOR

"I believe that God has created me and all that exists; that He has given and still preserves to me my body and soul, my eyes and ears, and all my members, my reason and all the powers of my soul."

In the beginning God created the heavens and the earth (Gen. 1:1).

God created the world by His word.

He spake, and it was done; He commanded, and it stood fast (Ps. 33:9)

1. THE ANGELS

We know nothing of the creation of the angels. The Bible tells that some of the angels sinned and that there are now good and evil angels. Of the good angels the Bible says,

Are they not all ministering spirits, sent forth to do service for the sake of them that shall inherit salvation? (Heb. 1:14.)

Of the evil angels we read,

Your adversary the devil, as a roaring lion, walketh about, seeking whom he may devour (I Pet. 5:8).

2. THE ORDER OF GOD'S WORK

The first chapter of Genesis tells how God the Father created the world. Having created the raw material (verses 1 and 2), God step by step made the earth suitable for the higher forms of life.

He created the forces that we call the laws of nature, the law of heredity, the law of gravity, and all the other laws of the universe.

God gave to His creation the joy of living. It is manifested in everything that breathes. He also decked nature in endless beauty of scenery, form, color, fragrance, and tune.

Having made the earth a suitable and good place to live in, God finally created man. This was the crowning act of God's creative work.

And God saw everything that He had made, and, behold, it was very good (Gen. 1:31).

3. THE IMAGE OF GOD

The Bible emphasizes the difference between man and animals by saying that God created man in His own image.

And God said, Let us make man in our image, after our likeness (Gen. 1:26).

And God created man in His own image, in the image of God created He him; male and female created He them (Gen. 1:27).

4. MAN AN INTELLECTUAL, MORAL, AND RELIGIOUS BEING

God created man an intellectual, moral, and religious being.

I. Man an intellectual being. As an intellectual being, man can work with ideas. The idea of a house or an automobile existed in somebody's mind even before the blueprints were drawn, let alone before it was built.

The ability to handle ideas makes man an explorer and inventor. He not only explores the forces of nature, but he also finds means to utilize these forces for his own benefit.

Man can also transmit his ideas and experiences to others. Thus, every generation builds on the work and experience of past generations.

Only man is equipped with such intellectual powers.

II. Man a moral being. As a moral being, man holds himself responsible to God for his acts. Man has a conscience. At a Bible camp a boy of fourteen promised to blow the

55

rising bugle at 6:45 in the morning. The responsibility for getting up on time was assumed by the boy, and he never failed. Every morning on the minute the lusty notes of the reveille aroused the camp to the activities of a new day.

We are facing responsibilities all along the road of life. Still, we would not live up to them unless we were created with a conscience that makes us feel it our duty to shoulder our responsibilities.

The ability and privilege to choose are a part of man's moral nature. Not only can he choose what to eat and where to go, but also between good and bad, right and wrong. Man has to decide as to what kind of life he wants to live.

Only man is thus endowed.

III. Man a religious being. As a religious being, man worships. The history of mankind is the history of religion. Man is the only being that builds altars. If he does not love and serve the true God, he loves and serves whatever seems to offer the help for the present and the hope for the future that his soul craves. When man tries to destroy his religious nature, he cripples himself.

Man is created for fellowship with God, and his soul is not at rest until it rests in God.

Only man is capable of such experiences.

God could not confer greater honor upon man than to create him in His own image. It is this image of God that constitutes man's soul and distinguishes him from the animals.

And man became a living soul (Gen. 2:7).

Thou hast made man but a little lower than God, and crownest him with glory and honor (Ps. 8:5).

5. THE IMAGE BEFORE THE FALL

As intellectual, moral, and religious persons, Adam and Eve had understanding, will, and conscience.

They were fully capable of understanding what God said to them. They were equally able to obey God. And peace and happiness filled their conscience, because they were in full harmony with God.

Created in the image of God, man was ready to take possession of the earth and to use all its riches according to the Creator's will.

56

Prayer:

I thank Thee, heavenly Father, that I am made in Thy likeness and that I am endowed with intellectual, moral, and religious powers. Help me as a child of Thine to use Thy gifts in love and obedience to Thee. Amen.

WORD STUDY

Reveille: the signal of a bugle or a drum to waken the camp in the morning.

QUESTIONS

(To be answered in writing, except 1 and 2)

1. Look up and read in your Bible the Bible passages quoted in this chapter. Underscore them in your Bible.
2. Be ready to recite the material that is to be memorized.
3. Our word can not create a plant or a flower or a bird or a fish. How then could God create the world by His word?
4. State (1) the work of the good angels and (2) of the evil angels.
5. How did the laws of nature originate?
6. Point out God's crowning work of creation.
7. Describe man's intellectual powers and state what these powers enable us to do.
8. As a moral being, what privileges does man possess and what responsibilities rest upon him?
9. State (1) how man's religious nature manifests itself and (2) the benefits and blessings it brings us if rightly used.
10. Point out the original condition of Adam's and Eve's (1) understanding, (2) will, and (3) conscience.
11. How can you prove that in Ps. 8:5, quoted in this chapter, David showed a better and truer knowledge of man than those who today say that man is but a highly developed animal?

BIBLE STUDY

After reading Gen. 1 point out (1) the progressive order of God's creative work; (2) how often it is said, "And God saw it was good," and the meaning of these words; (3) the use of the term, "After its kind," and the meaning of this term; (4) the difference between the plan followed in verses 24 and 25 and the one followed in verses 26 and 27; (5) the position man was to hold in the earth; (6) the picture this chapter gives (1) of God, and (2) of man.

CHAPTER FOURTEEN

The First Article --

GOD'S CARE FOR THE WORLD

Adam and Eve were created without sin. They feared, loved and trusted God. But they were not self-sufficient. It was true then as it is now that "in Him we live and move and have our being" (Acts 17:28).

Besides other necessities, God furnished the truth that should guide them, inspired the will to glad obedience, and as a result filled them with peace and joy. As long as they trusted God, He could share all these things with them.

1. SIN ENTERS

We know how the devil's lie led Adam and Eve to distrust God and disobey Him. They sinned. The disobedience brought quick and fearful disaster. They died as God had told them they would. Their childlike fear of God died, their love of Him died, their faith in Him died. Dreading to meet God, they hid themselves. They were still intellectual, moral, and religious beings, but it was already evident that their understanding had been darkened, their will corrupted, and their conscience filled with terror. And evil desires had taken possession of them. The old Adam, as the corrupted nature is called, had appeared.

2. WE INHERIT SIN

The destructive influence of sin did not stop with Adam and Eve. The Bible significantly says, "Adam begat a son in his own likeness, after his image" (Gen. 5:3).

58

Adam and Eve passed on their corrupted nature to their children. This is what we call inherited or original sin.

Through one man sin entered into the world, and death through sin; and so death passed unto all men, for that all sinned (Rom. 5:12).

3. AGAIN GOD'S LOVE ACTS

The creation of Adam and Eve was an act of love. When they sinned, God again proved His love. He punished them for their disobedience, for they had to learn to repent of their sin, but He also promised to send a Savior who would save them from the power of the devil.

Adam and Eve had other needs. Sin had brought sickness, let loose hatred and evil lusts, and exposed them to danger and death. They needed to be preserved, to be provided for, and to be guarded and kept from all evil.

They did not deserve that God should do all this for them any more than they deserved that He should send the Savior. Still, so great was God's fatherly goodness and mercy that even sin could not stop Him from taking care of them.

What God did for Adam and Eve He does for me. He does not change, and He loves me as He loved them.

4. GOD PRESERVES AND PROVIDES

I. *"I believe that God . . . preserves to me my body and soul, my eyes and ears, and all my members, my reason and all the powers of my soul, together with food and raiment, home and family, and all my property."*

Nothing is lacking. I can speak to Him about every one of these needs and trust Him to hear me and to take care of me.

Your heavenly Father knoweth that ye have need of all these things (Matt. 6:32).

And God is not stingy. *"He daily provides abundantly for all the needs of my life."*

The eyes of all wait for Thee, and Thou givest them their food in due season (Ps. 145:15).

Do not overlook the word "needs." There is a great difference between what I need and what I may want. At times I even need what I do not want. Like all others, I need to learn what the great apostle practiced: "Having food and covering we shall be therewith content" (I Tim. 6:8).

II. God also preserves the world He created. He controls and uses the laws of nature. He holds the stars in His hands and the years and seasons obey His will.

While the earth remaineth, seedtime and harvest, and cold and heat, and summer and winter, and day and night shall not cease (Gen. 8:22).

5. GOD PROTECTS

"I believe that God . . . protects me from all danger, and guards and keeps me from all evil."

I do not always understand His ways. Sickness, suffering, and sorrow come to me as to others. Violent disturbances of nature and horrors of war may some day be my personal experience. Still I believe that my heavenly Father protects me from all danger and guards me from all evil. I believe it because I know I can trust my Father in heaven. He knows what His child needs in order to grow into Christian manhood and usefulness, and

We know that to them that love God all things work together for good (Rom. 8:28).

Besides, the word stands fast that

He that keepeth thee will not slumber (Ps. 121:3).

6. WE SHOULD THANK GOD

"For all which I am in duty bound to thank, praise, serve, and obey Him."

Oh, give thanks unto the Lord; for He is good; for His lovingkindness endureth forever (Ps. 106:1).

Words of thanks and praise must and will flow from a thankful heart. But I will not use words alone. I will also serve and obey Him or my words are merely empty sounds. Therefore, I will use my body and soul, my eyes and ears, and all my members in His service, and my property, too. Then my whole life will be a thank-offering to my heavenly Father for His goodness.

It is most certainly true that God the Father Almighty has created me, preserves me, provides for me, protects me, and guards and keeps me. May it also be most certainly true that I will thank Him, praise Him, and serve and obey Him every day of my life.

Prayer:

I thank Thee, my God and Father, for life and home and food and clothes and the many other things that I need. Make me truly grateful and obedient to Thee. I rejoice that Jesus Christ came to save me from my sin. Help me to trust and love Him. Keep and guard my dear ones and all Thy people. Protect my country from evil and teach the people to use Thy gifts according to Thy will. In Jesus' name. Amen.

WORD STUDY

Self-sufficient: able to supply themselves with everything they needed. Corrupted: ruined and perverted by sin. Raiment: clothing.

QUESTIONS

(To be answered in writing, except 1 and 2)

1. Look up and read in your Bible the Bible passages quoted in this chapter. Underscore them in your Bible.
2. Be ready to recite the material that is to be memorized.
3. How were Adam and Eve dependent upon God before the fall?
4. What did sin do to (1) their understanding, (2) their will, and (3) their conscience?
5. What else did sin do to them?
6. Explain inherited or original sin.
7. How did God show them His love after the fall?
8. Make a list of things God must preserve.
9. State the difference between what we need and what we may want.
10. Make a list of what you have received from God that you cannot buy at the stores.
11. What is God's relation to the world He created?
12. Why should you thank and praise God?
13. In what ways should you thank and praise Him?
14. Why are these words added: This is most certainly true?
15. Stephen, Peter, Paul and many others have been put to death for confessing Christ. How do you harmonize this fact with the faith you confess in the First Article?
16. Of what value to you in your daily life is the faith you confess in the First Article?

BIBLE STUDY

After reading Acts 27, point out (1) where the voyage took place; (2) the route of the ship; (3) the four times Paul gave advice during the journey; (4) what he advised each time; (5) how the advice was received; (6) what was the source of Paul's confidence and courage; (7) what moved Paul, facing certain shipwreck, to do what is told in v. 35; (8) why God did not spare His servant from the hardship and dangers of being shipwrecked.

61

CHAPTER FIFTEEN

The Second Article - - of Redemption

I believe in Jesus Christ, His only Son, our Lord; who was conceived by the Holy Ghost, born of the Virgin Mary; suffered under Pontius Pilate, was crucified, dead, and buried; He descended into hell; the third day He rose again from the dead; He ascended into heaven, and sitteth on the right hand of God the Father Almighty; from thence He shall come to judge the quick and the dead.

What does this mean?

Answer: I believe that Jesus Christ, true God, begotten of the Father from eternity, and also true Man, born of the Virgin Mary, is my Lord;

who has redeemed me, a lost and condemned creature, bought me and freed me from all sins, from death, and from the power of the devil;

not with silver and gold, but with His holy and precious blood, and with His innocent sufferings and death;

in order that I might be His own, live under Him in His kingdom, and serve Him in everlasting righteousness, innocence, and blessedness;

even as He is risen from the dead, and lives and reigns to all eternity. This is most certainly true.

JESUS CHRIST TRUE GOD AND TRUE MAN

In the Second Article I confess my faith in Jesus Christ, true God and true man.

1. CHRIST'S COMING FORETOLD

The plan to send Christ to save man from sin came from God. He revealed His plan immediately after the fall of Adam and Eve.

I will put enmity between thee [the devil] *and the woman, and between thy seed and her seed; He shall bruise thy head, and thou shalt bruise His heel* (Gen. 3:15).

Without this promise there would have been no salvation for Adam and Eve. The people of the Old Testament were saved by faith in the Christ that was to come. The people of the New Testament are saved by faith in the Christ that has come.

During the Old Testament time God repeated the promise of a Savior and made the promise more and more plain and definite.[1]

2. THE FULNESS OF THE TIME

Christ came in "the fulness of the time," that is, the time when the preparatory work for His coming had been completed within Israel and when the conditions outside of Israel were ripe for the spreading of the gospel.

When the fulness of the time came, God sent forth His Son, born of a woman (Gal. 4:4).

3. HIS NAMES

My Savior's full name is Jesus Christ; Jesus is His personal name and means Savior.

Thou shalt call His name Jesus: for it is He that shall save His people from their sins (Matt. 1:21).

Christ means the anointed, the same as Messiah. This name identifies Him as the promised Messiah.

We have found the Messiah which is, being interpreted, Christ (John 1:41).

4. JESUS CHRIST TRUE GOD

"I believe that Jesus Christ is true God, begotten of the Father from eternity."

---

[1]Christ was to be a descendant of Abraham (Gen. 12:3), of the tribe of Judah (Gen. 49:10), a ruler and king (Num. 24:17), a prophet like Moses (Deut. 18:15), a priest and king like Melchizedek (Ps. 110:4 and Zech. 6:13), a son of David (II Sam. 7:16 and Ps. 110:1), born in Bethlehem and yet being from eternity (Mi. 5:2), born of a virgin (Is. 7:14) and the Son of God (Ps. 2:7). He was to suffer and die for our sin (Is. 53:4-5), be buried in a rich man's grave (Is. 53:9), bring salvation to the end of the earth (Is. 49:6), and rule forever (Dan. 7:13-14).

There are four reasons why I believe that Jesus Christ is true God.

I. God calls Him His beloved Son.

This is my beloved Son in whom I am well pleased (Matt. 3:17 and 17:5).

II. Jesus Himself declares,

I and the Father are one (John 10:30).

III. His life was sinless and holy. Christ was as different from sinful man as only God can be. He fulfilled God's will both in letter and in spirit.

Jesus loved and trusted God as He should be loved and trusted. He also loved His neighbor as Himself, nay, even more than Himself. In this world of ours such perfection is not human. It is divine.

Which of you convicteth Me of sin? (John 8:46.)

IV. The apostle states that

Jesus Christ was declared to be the Son of God with power . . . by the resurrection from the dead (Rom. 1:4).

5. JESUS CHRIST TRUE MAN

"I believe that Jesus Christ . . . is also true man, born of the Virgin Mary."

He was born of a woman and grew and developed like any other child. "Jesus advanced in wisdom and stature, and in favor with God and men" (Luke 2:52).

He found it necessary to eat and sleep, He became tired (John 4:6) and He suffered and died. In fact, He was a man such as God intended each of us to be. Again the apostle declares,

There is one God, one mediator also between God and man, Himself man, Christ Jesus (I Tim. 2:5).

6. CONCEIVED BY THE HOLY SPIRIT

"I believe in Jesus Christ . . . who was conceived by the Holy Ghost."

How could Jesus Christ be both God and man? The Bible answers, He was conceived by the Holy Spirit. The angel Gabriel said to Mary: "Behold, thou shalt conceive in thy womb, and bring forth a son. . . . The Holy Spirit shall come upon thee, and the power of the Most High shall overshadow thee, wherefore also the holy thing which is

64

begotten shall be called the Son of God" (Luke 1:31 and 35).

How Christ could become man is a complete mystery to me. I thank God that He has not told me to understand Jesus Christ in order to be saved, but to trust and obey Him. If that were not so, there would be no salvation for me.

Prayer:

Glory and praise be to Thee, my heavenly Father, that Thou didst love fallen men so that Thou didst send Thy Son to save us. And with my whole heart I praise Thee, Jesus Christ, who art able and worthy to be my Savior and Lord, my Redeemer and God. Help me to trust Thee and to love and serve Thee. Amen.

WORD STUDY

Redemption: deliverance, rescue, salvation.

QUESTIONS

(To be answered in writing, except 1 and 2)

1. Look up and read in your Bible the Bible passages quoted in this chapter. Underscore them in your Bible.
2. Be ready to recite the material that is to be memorized.
3. In whom do you believe, according to the Second Article?
4. When was Christ's coming first foretold?
5. Of what value was this promise to the people of those early days?
6. How were the people of the Old Testament times saved?
7. Read in your Bible the passages given in the footnote and note what is said of Christ in each passage.
8. State the meaning of "the fulness of the time."
9. Give the meaning of (1) Jesus and (2) Christ.
10. State your reasons for believing that Jesus Christ is true God.
11. Why do you believe that Jesus Christ is true man?
12. How could one born of a woman be true God?
13. What makes it more difficult to understand Christ than to understand any other person?
14. How much has our understanding of the person Jesus Christ to do with our salvation?
15. State the difference between knowing Christ and understanding Christ.
16. Who are saved by Christ?

BIBLE STUDY

1. After reading (1) John 8:58; (2) John 17:5; (3) Matt. 18:20; and (4) Matt. 28:18, point out what attribute Jesus ascribes to Himself in each of these passages.
2. Read John 13:1-11 and state what this story reveals of the character of Jesus.
3. After reading John 20:26-29, explain what caused the doubting Thomas to believe that Jesus was God.

CHAPTER SIXTEEN

The Second Article --

THE REDEEMER

The work of the Redeemer had been outlined in the Old Testament. It was there that Jesus Christ found His program, every detail of which He fulfilled. According to the Old Testament He was to do the work of a prophet, a priest, and a king.

1. CHRIST REVEALS THE FATHER

For centuries God had spoken to the Israelites through the prophets, but even so it was an incomplete knowledge they had of God the Father. God could not make Himself fully known through persons who were sinners, even though they were prophets. Only the Son could fully reveal the Father, because He alone came from God. He alone had the Son's knowledge of the Father, and He alone could say:

He that hath seen Me hath seen the Father (John 14:9).

Christ Himself pointed out how dependent all men are upon Him for their knowledge of the Father.

Neither doth any know the Father, save the Son, and he to whomsoever the Son willeth to reveal Him (Matt. 11:27).

Christ furnished all the knowledge of God that either the individual or the whole human family is able to absorb and make use of in this life. His words are therefore my highest authority in all questions concerning what to believe and how to live in order to be saved

This is called Christ's prophetic work.

2. CHRIST HAS REDEEMED ME

We come now to Christ's work as priest and mediator.

"I believe that Jesus Christ . . . has redeemed me, a lost and condemned creature, bought me and freed me from all sins, and death, and from the power of the devil."

There are three forces that rule over all those whom Christ has not personally redeemed: sin, death, and the devil. From these unholy powers Christ has redeemed me and all who believe in Him and have been baptized into His name.

3. CHRIST HAS REDEEMED ME FROM SIN

Christ has redeemed me from the guilt and the eternal punishment of my sins.

By fulfilling the law in my behalf and by paying the penalty of all my sins, Christ has taken away the condemnation that my sins had brought upon me. In Him I have the forgiveness of all my sins.

Christ has also broken the hold sin has upon me.

There is in every man an inborn love of sinning. I find this evil love in myself. I love to do my own will and to hear my own praises sung. There is something in me that likes to listen to the sugared voice of the tempter.

Dora had been naughty the whole evening. Praying her evening prayers, she had finished the memorized prayers and started an addition in her own words. Her father suggested: Dear Jesus, make Dora a good and obedient girl. Dora paid no attention. Father repeated the suggestion, but she kept up her stream of words. Again the suggestion was repeated. "I don't want to say that," she flashed back. "Why not?" "Because some times I want to be good and some times I want to be mean."

It is the "wanting to be mean" that causes so much trouble. Only Christ is able to overcome this stubborn and evil will. But I must confess it to Him and earnestly ask Him to take it away from me. Only then can His Holy Spirit do the necessary work in any heart. He will enable me to fight against the wicked lust. The Spirit will renew my love of my Lord and Savior, make me hate the sin that cost Him so much, and give me power to walk with Christ.

Being made free from sin and become servants to God, ye have your fruit unto sanctification, and the end eternal life (Rom. 6:22) .

There is therefore now no condemnation to them that are in Christ Jesus (Rom. 8:1) . (See Chap. Twenty-six, 7.)

4. CHRIST HAS REDEEMED ME FROM DEATH

Death is another cruel master. It came upon Adam and Eve when they sinned. Their trust in God as well as their love for Him died, and fear and dread took their place. The death of the body followed and from Adam death passed unto all men. When the body dies, the soul that is without Christ goes into a dark and hopeless eternity.

When Christ rose from the dead, He made eternal life a certainty for His followers. He took away the dark dread with which death had filled human life. With Christ the grave becomes a resting place for the body, the soul goes home to God, and on the resurrection morning the body shall arise and we shall always be with the Lord.

Death is swallowed up in victory (I Cor. 15:54) .

5. CHRIST HAS REDEEMED ME FROM THE POWER OF THE DEVIL

Before the coming of Christ, Satan ruled undisputedly in the nations outside of Israel. Only by becoming a member of Israel could a Gentile become a member of the kingdom of heaven here on earth.

Christ changed this situation. He defeated Satan in the temptations, on the cross, and on Easter morning. He gave to His church the saving means of grace, the Word and the Sacraments, and He gave the believers the Holy Spirit. In addition, He promised to be present among His own wherever they gathered in the use of the means of grace and in prayer, a promise He has faithfully kept. And He added that no one should snatch His own out of His hand or out of His Father's hand.

Since then the kingdom of heaven has been in worldwide activity. The believers everywhere are protected by Christ against the snares of the devil so long as they use the means of grace and trust and follow Him.

Thanks be to God, who giveth us the victory through our Lord Jesus Christ (I Cor. 15:57) .

And now I have the privilege of having Jesus Christ as my Lord and Master. I belong to Him and do not want any other lord.

68

Prayer:

> I thank Thee, uncreated Sun,
> That Thy bright beams on me have shined;
> I thank Thee, who hast overthrown
> My foes, and healed my wounded mind;
> I thank Thee, whose enlivening voice
> Bids my freed heart in Thee rejoice. Amen.

(L. H. No. 474, v. 2)

QUESTIONS
(To be answered in writing, except 1 and 2)

1. Look up and read in your Bible the Bible passages quoted in this chapter. Underscore them in your Bible.
2. Be ready to recite the material that is to be memorized.
3. How was the work of Christ outlined in the Old Testament?
4. What is Christ's prophetic work?
5. Why could Christ reveal God more fully than the prophets?
6. What did Christ mean when He said: "He that hath seen Me hath seen the Father"?
7. State why the words of Christ, to a Christian, are the highest authority in matters of faith and life.
8. What makes sin rule in the heart that does not love Christ?
9. Give evidences of the rule of sin in such hearts.
10. What is Christ's priestly work?
11. How has Christ redeemed me from the power of sin?
12. And from the condemnation of sin?
13. What died in Adam's and Eve's hearts when they sinned?
14. What took its place?
15. Why do we call death a cruel master?
16. How has Christ redeemed me from death?
17. How could a Gentile become a member of the kingdom of heaven before the coming of Christ?
18. Point out the changes brought by Christ.
19. State how Christ has redeemed me from the power of the devil.

BIBLE STUDY

1. After reading Heb. 1:1-4, point out (1) by whom God spoke to the fathers of old; (2) the meaning of "by divers portions and in divers manners"; (3) by whom He has spoken "at the end of these days"; (4) the eight characteristics ascribed to this spokesman in verses 2 to 4.

2. Read Heb. 2:14-15 and state (1) who are the children in verse 14; (2) what is said of them; (3) the reason Christ took on flesh and blood; (4) His purpose in so doing; (5) the means He used to accomplish the purpose; (6) who had the power of death; (7) the meaning of "the power of death"; and (8) the effect the fear of death had upon men.

69

CHAPTER SEVENTEEN

The Second Article --

JESUS CHRIST THE SUFFERING SAVIOR

"I believe that Jesus Christ ... has bought me and freed me ... not with silver and gold, but with His holy and precious blood, and with His innocent sufferings and death."

We continue the study of Christ's priestly work.

1. THE OLD TESTAMENT TYPE

The Old Testament priest was the mediator between God and man. He alone could officiate at the altar of Jehovah and bring to Him the sacrifices of the people. The chief of the priests was called the high priest. On the day of atonement, when a sacrifice was brought for the sins of the whole nation, he went into the Holy of Holies of the sanctuary and sprinkled the sacrificial blood on the mercy seat, the cover of the ark of the covenant. He brought back to the waiting people Jehovah's blessing, called the Aaronic blessing, assuring them of the forgiveness of their sin and of God's love.

The high priest was a type and a prophecy of Christ, the true high priest and mediator between God and man. "Having then a great high priest, . . . Jesus the Son of God, let us hold fast our confession" (Heb. 4:14).

2. THE LAW OF SUBSTITUTION

The Old Testament sin offerings brought to the Lord by the priests on behalf of the people were based on the law of substitution. The animal took the place of the sinner whose sins were transferred to the animal by the laying of hands upon its head.

The law of substitution is as universal as life itself. Christ pointed to this fact when He said: "Except a grain of wheat fall into the earth and die, it abideth by itself alone; but if it die, it beareth much fruit" (John 12:24)

In all spheres of life one sacrifices for the benefit of another. The best we have in home, church, and state is paid for by the labor, sufferings, and even death of those that preceded us.

When Christ became man He took the place of the sinner to do for him what the sinner could not do for himself.

3. CHRIST THE FULFILLER OF THE LAW

Christ fulfilled the law that I have broken. He could not plead my case before God unless He, in every respect, had fulfilled the law in my behalf. Therefore, He said: *Think not that I came to destroy the law or the prophets; I came not to destroy, but to fulfill* (Matt. 5:17).

4. CHRIST THE SIN BEARER

God laid our sins upon Him, and willingly and gladly did He bear them.

His own self bare our sins in His own body upon the tree (I Peter 2:24).

Christ redeemed us from the curse of the law, having become a curse for us; for it is written, Cursed is every one that hangeth on a tree (Gal. 3:13)

So fully did Christ take the place of us all, that His death has the same effect as if every one had died for his own sin.

We thus judge that one died for all, therefore all died; and He died for all (II Cor. 5:14-15).

5. ON THE CROSS

It was a part of "the fulness of the time" (Gal. 4:4) that the Romans ruled over Palestine when Jesus was crucified. Pontius Pilate was Roman governor over Judea. Jesus Christ was crucified under Roman law, not under the Mosaic law. The Mosaic law provided that the body of one who had been put to death, might afterwards be hung on a tree in order to emphasize the shameful character of the crime committed (Deut. 21:22-23) . The Romans crucified people alive.

Christ demonstrated even in the manner in which He died that He took upon Himself the curse of the most shameful and degrading sin. No sinner, not even the greatest, should ever be able to face Christ and say: You did not die for my sins.

When Jesus Christ died after being on the cross for about six hours, it was because He Himself gave up His spirit to the Father. His was a voluntary sacrifice from first to last.

And Jesus, crying with a loud voice, said, Father, into Thy hands I commend My spirit; and having said this, He gave up the ghost (Luke 23:46) .

Unspeakable as the physical sufferings were, His spiritual sufferings were even greater. He knew His road led through Gethsemane to Golgotha and He was prepared for what was in store for Him. Still, prepared though He was, the anguish of soul in the garden forced the blood to mix with the sweat and made Him ask thrice: *My Father, if it be possible, let this cup pass away from Me* (Matt. 26:39) .

On the cross, He, the Son, cried to His Father:

My God, My God, why hast Thou forsaken Me? (Matt. 27:46) .

Truly, here is spiritual suffering that no human mind can grasp.

Then when Christ had emptied the cup of sufferings, He said:

It is finished (John 19:30) .

Yes, finished were the sufferings for my sins. The sacrifice had been brought and the forgiveness of sin had been won.

Prayer:

What language shall I borrow
To thank Thee, dearest Friend,
For this Thy dying sorrow,
For pity without end?
Oh, make me Thine forever;
And, should I fainting be,
Lord, let me never, never,
Outlive my love to Thee. Amen
(L. H. No. 315, v. 6)

WORD STUDY

Type: model, pattern. Mediator: one who intercedes or pleads in behalf of another. Substitution: taking the place and acting in behalf of another. Universal: general, common.

QUESTIONS

(To be answered in writing, except 1 and 2)

1. Look up and read in your Bible the Bible passages quoted in this chapter. Underscore them in your Bible.
2. Be ready to recite the material that is to be memorized.
3. How was the high priest a type of Christ?
4. State the law of substitution as it operated in the Old Testament sacrifices.
5. How universal is this law?
6. Give a list of benefits we enjoy as a result of this law.
7. Explain how none lives to himself and none dies to himself.
8. How did the law of substitution apply to Jesus Christ?
9. Why was it necessary that Christ fulfil the law in our behalf?
10. Who made Christ the sin bearer?
11. How did He redeem us from the curse of the law?
12. Under what law was Christ crucified?
13. State the difference between Mosaic and Roman law regarding the hanging of a person on a tree.
14. What evidence do we have of Christ's spiritual sufferings?
15. State Paul's meaning when he says that Christ died for all, therefore all died.
16. What did Christ mean when He said: "It is finished"?

BIBLE STUDY

Read Isaiah 53 and (1) state of whom the prophet speaks; (2) make a list of this person's burdens and sufferings; (3) point out what people thought of Him; (4) describe how He Himself behaved; (5) make a list of the benefits produced by His sufferings.

CHAPTER EIGHTEEN

The Second Article --

JESUS CHRIST RISEN FROM THE DEAD

The body of Jesus was buried in a rock-hewn new grave belonging to Joseph of Arimathea, a rich member of the high council. He had been a secret believer in Jesus. Isaiah had prophesied that Christ should be "with a rich man in His death" (Is. 53:9), and the Scriptures were fulfilled to the smallest details.

1. CHRIST DESCENDED INTO HELL

We now begin our study of Christ's work as king.

We follow Him on a journey that is beyond the experience of living men.

"Christ also suffered for sins once . . . being put to death in the flesh, but made alive in the spirit; in which also He went and preached unto the spirits in prison, that aforetime were disobedient, when the longsuffering of God waited in the days of Noah" (I Peter 3:18-20).

Christ went where the rebellious generation of Noah's days was imprisoned. In the New Testament this prison is called both hades and hell. It is the special kingdom of Satan.

The word translated "preached" really means "proclaimed." It was His victory over sin, death, and Satan that Christ proclaimed. Even in hell Christ demonstrated His victory by entering and leaving the devil's stronghold at will. The word does not imply any preaching of the gospel or a second chance for those who are lost.

2. CHRIST ROSE FROM THE DEAD

On Easter Sunday, the third day after His death, Christ rose from the dead. His body, though the same, was now a spiritual body. What a spiritual body is, we do not know. It is one of God's many mysteries that we shall know when on the resurrection day we, too, shall have spiritual bodies. *The Lord is risen indeed* (Luke 24:34).

3. THE DISCIPLES DID NOT EXPECT CHRIST TO RISE

Christ had repeatedly told His disciples that He should die, and rise again on the third day. Still, they did not believe Him. They could not see that His death and resurrection were necessary for our salvation. After His crucifixion they did not expect to see Him alive again.

The two on the Emmaus road did not recognize Christ. They told Him: "Certain women of our company amazed us . . . saying, that they had also seen a vision of angels, who said that He was alive" (Luke 24:22-23).

In the evening of the same day—Easter Sunday—when Christ suddenly stood in the midst of the disciples, we are told that "they were terrified and affrighted, and supposed that they beheld a spirit" (Luke 24:37).

When Thomas was told by the other disciples that Christ had risen and that they had seen Him, he stubbornly declared: "Except I shall see in His hands the print of the nails, and put my finger into the print of the nails, and put my hand into His side, I will not believe" (John 20:25).

4. CHRIST CONVINCED HIS DOUBTING DISCIPLES

During the forty days after His resurrection, Christ demonstrated to His friends that He really and truly was risen from the dead. This He did by showing Himself to them many times and under varied circumstances. Paul gives us a list of six appearances (I Cor. 15:5-8), and the gospels record at least six more.[1] In this way Christ built in the disciples an unshakeable certainty that He, their Lord and Savior, was truly alive.

---

[1] The appearances were: (1) to Mary Magdalene (Mark 16:9, John 20:11-18); (2) to several women (Matt. 28:9-10, Luke 24:10); (3) to Peter (Luke 24:34); (4) to the two on the Emmaus road (Luke 24:13-35); (5) to the disciples, Thomas not being present (Luke 24:36-43); (6) to the eleven (John 20:26-29); (7) to more than five hundred (I Cor. 15:6); (8) to some of the disciples at the Sea of Galilee (John 21:1-14); (9) to James (I Cor. 15:7); (10) to the eleven on a mountain in Galilee (Matt. 28:16-20); (11) to the disciples when He ascended into heaven (Luke 24:50-53); (12) to Paul (I Cor. 15:8).

Thomas is a good example. Eight days after Easter the disciples were together and Thomas with them. Suddenly Jesus stood in the midst of them and said to Thomas: "Reach hither thy finger, and see my hands; and reach hither thy hand, and put it into My side: and be not faithless, but believing." All doubt vanished. The Lord was risen indeed.

Thomas answered and said unto Him, My Lord and my God (John 20:28).

5. WHAT CHRIST'S RESURRECTION MEANS TO ME

The resurrection proved that Jesus Christ is God's Son and Himself God. (See Thomas' answer and Chapter Fifteen, 4, IV). When I trust in Jesus Christ, I know I trust in God. What God can do, Jesus Christ can do, and so I know I have a Savior who is fully able to take care of me.

His resurrection brought other benefits to me. The power that raised Christ from the dead is at work in all who believe in the risen Savior. In this power, I, too, as a follower of Jesus Christ may live the new life of God's children.

As Christ was raised from the dead through the glory of the Father, so we also might walk in newness of life (Rom. 6:4).

The resurrection brought me still another benefit. The fact that Christ rose from the dead guarantees the resurrection of the dead. As Christ lives and reigns to all eternity so I, too, as His disciple shall live and serve Him in everlasting righteousness, innocence, and blessedness.

For as in Adam all die, so also in Christ shall all be made alive (I Cor. 15:22).

The risen Christ shall fulfil His majestic words: *I am the resurrection and the life; he that believeth on Me, though he die, yet shall he live; and whosoever liveth and believeth on Me shall never die* (John 11:25-26).

6. CHRIST ASCENDED INTO HEAVEN TO PREPARE A PLACE FOR ME

Christ promised His disciples: *In My Father's house are many mansions; if it were not so, I would have told you; for I go to prepare a place for you* (John 14:2).

So I know where my Savior went when He, on Ascension

day, entered into heaven. And I know where I am going. Glory be to His name!

Prayer:

> For the joy Thy birth doth give me,
> For Thy holy, precious Word;
> For Thy Baptism which does save me,
> For Thy gracious Festal Board;
> For Thy death, the bitter scorn,
> For Thy resurrection morn,
> Lord, I thank Thee and extol Thee,
> And in heaven I shall behold Thee. Amen.
>
> (L. H. No. 325, v. 10)

QUESTIONS

(To be answered in writing, except 1 and 2)

1. Look up and read in your Bible the Bible passages quoted in this chapter. Underscore them in your Bible.
2. Be ready to recite the material that is to be memorized.
3. In whose grave was Jesus buried?
4. How were the Scriptures fulfilled at His burial?
5. State (1) the New Testament names of the prison spoken of in I Peter 3:19-20; (2) the conditions in this prison; and (3) the ruler of the prison.
6. Why did Christ go to this prison?
7. What did the disciples think of Jesus' words that He should rise on the third day?
8. Give examples showing that they did not expect Him to rise from the dead.
9. How did Christ convince them that He was risen?
10. What did Christ do in the case of Thomas?
11. List the benefits that have come to you as a result of Christ's resurrection.
12. What did Christ say about His Father's house?
13. What was He going to do there?
14. When did He go to this house?
15. What help is it to you that He went to His Father's house?

BIBLE STUDY

1. Read Is. 53:9; Matt. 27:38; and Matt. 27:57-60; and point out how the prophecy of Isaiah was fulfilled.
2. After reading Luke 24:13-43, point out (1) why these two men were leaving Jerusalem; (2) in what state of mind they were; (3) how Jesus opened the conversation; (4) why He wanted them to talk first; (5) what means He used to straighten out their thinking; (6) the effect His words had upon them; (7) how they knew Him; (8) why they returned to Jerusalem; (9) what happened when they came back to Jerusalem.
3. Read Luke 24:50-53 and state (1) the last thing Jesus did before He left His disciples; (2) what the disciples did after they had seen Him ascend into heaven; (3) in what frame of mind they returned to Jerusalem.

CHAPTER NINETEEN

The Second Article - -

JESUS CHRIST AT THE RIGHT HAND OF GOD

"I believe that Jesus Christ . . . sitteth on the right hand of God the Father Almighty; from thence He shall come to judge the quick and the dead."
To sit at the right hand of God the Father means that Jesus Christ, the God-man, has the same authority, power, and honor that God has.
Jesus Christ is on the right hand of God, having gone into heaven; angels and authorities and powers being made subject unto Him (I Peter 3:22).

1. JESUS CHRIST INTERCEDES FOR ME

He uses His power and authority to finish the work that He began here on earth. There are two sides to Christ's work at the right hand of God. The one is that He acts as a mediator for me and for all who honestly plead God's forgiveness for their sins for Christ's sake. The other is that He protects me and all believers against our enemies.

When I approach God, confessing my sins and asking forgiveness, Christ is there with His blood blotting out my sins. Since His blood cleanses from all sins, there is always forgiveness for me with God.

Who is he that condemneth? It is Christ Jesus that died, yea rather, that was raised from the dead, who is at the right hand of God, who also maketh intercession for us (Rom. 8:34).

He is able to save to the uttermost them that draw near unto God through Him, seeing He ever liveth to make intercession for them (Heb. 7:25).

2. JESUS CHRIST IS RULER AND KING

His other work at the right hand of God consists in this that He protects me and all believers against our enemies.

Using the illustration of the shepherd and his sheep Jesus said, "My sheep hear My voice, and I know them, and they follow Me; and I give unto them eternal life; and they shall never perish, and no one shall snatch them out of My hand" (John 10:27-28).

This promise Christ fulfills every day. My own evil lusts and the evil influences of others are constantly at work to destroy my trust in my Savior and my love and obedience to Him.

> Stood we alone in our own might,
> Our striving would be losing;
> For us the one true man doth fight,
> The man of God's own choosing.
> Who is this chosen One?
> 'Tis Jesus Christ, the Son,
> The Lord of hosts, 'tis He
> Who wins the victory
> In every field of battle.
> (L. H., No. 270, v. 2)

So I trust Him and pray that He will keep me close to Himself in the Word and the Sacraments within the holy Christian Church. I know He will keep His promise.

"These shall war against the Lamb, and the Lamb shall overcome them, for He is Lord of lords and King of kings" (Rev. 17:14). "And He hath on His garment and on His thigh a name written, KING OF KINGS, AND LORD OF LORDS" (Rev. 19:16).

He shall reign for ever and ever (Rev. 11:15).

3. JESUS CHRIST IS THE JUDGE OF THE QUICK AND THE DEAD

Judgment is necessary in this world of sin. Good and evil must be separated if there is to be salvation, and judgment is one of the means God uses to bring about the separation. Through the conscience, God judges us when we have done wrong. He calls us to repent and to turn to Him.

In the history of the nations, there are special seasons or periods of judgment. The world wars were such periods. Nations and their rulers had counseled together to break the Lord's commandments (Ps. 2). Their sins brought wars and unspeakable sufferings. It was God's way to judge the nations and to call them to repentance. Judgment day will see the last and final act of the drama in human history.

"When the Son of man shall come in His glory, and all the angels with Him, then shall He sit on the throne of His glory; and before Him shall be gathered all the nations; and He shall separate them one from another" (Matt. 25: 31-32). "Then shall the King say unto them on His right hand, Come ye blessed of my Father, inherit the kingdom prepared for you from the foundation of the world" (Matt. 25:34). "Then shall He say also unto them on the left hand, Depart from Me, ye cursed, into the eternal fire which is prepared for the devil and his angels" (Matt. 25:41). "And these shall go away into eternal punishment, but the righteous into eternal life" (Matt. 25:46).

In that gathering you and I will be; we will either be invited to come or told to depart.

4. CHRIST SHALL JUDGE ACCORDING TO HIS WORD

Christ will judge the quick and the dead according to His own word.

No matter how influential a man has been in this world or how much he has been praised by men, his word will carry no weight before the judgment seat of Christ. On that day the words of Him who is Savior, Lord, and Judge will be final.

The word that I spake, the same shall judge him in the last day (John 12:48).

5. THAT I MIGHT BE HIS OWN

"I believe that Jesus Christ ... has redeemed me ... in order that I might be His own, live under Him in His kingdom, and serve Him in everlasting righteousness, innocence, and blessedness; even as He is risen from the dead, and lives and reigns to all eternity. This is most certainly true."

This is another privilege that Christ has won for me. It was the purpose of His coming to this world that I might be set free from sin to serve Him and to live and reign with Him to all eternity. (See Chap. Sixteen, 3.)

Christ gave Himself for us, that He might redeem us from all iniquity, and purify unto Himself a people for His own possession, zealous of good works (Titus 2:14).

Prayer:

I thank Thee, Lord Jesus Christ, for Thy victory over Satan, sin, and death. Thy victory is my victory. I rejoice that Thou art King of kings and Lord of lords, and that Thou always art with me and all Thy friends. Anew I pledge my allegiance to Thee. Help me to grow in the grace and knowledge of Thee. Lord, make Thy victory known throughout the world. Help that the number of those who accept Thee as Lord and Savior may grow ever more. Let Thy kingdom come and Thy will be done on earth as it is in heaven. Amen.

WORD STUDY

Intercede: to act as a mediator, to plead in behalf of another.
Drama: a series of forceful, impressive actions.

QUESTIONS
(To be answered in writing, except 1 and 2)

1. Look up and read in your Bible the Bible passages quoted in this chapter. Underscore them in your Bible.
2. Be ready to recite the material that is to be memorized.
3. What does it mean that Christ "sitteth at the right hand of God"?
4. Point out the two sides of the work Christ is doing at the right hand of the Father.
5. Explain His intercession.
6. What is Christ's work as king?
7. Who are our spiritual enemies?
8. What is their aim?
9. Why can Christ defend us against these enemies?
10. What means has He given us to use against them?
11. Why is judgment necessary?
12. State God's purpose with judgments during the time of grace.
13. What will happen in the last judgment?
14. Explain the use Christ will make of His word in that judgment.
15. For what purpose did Christ redeem you?
16. Why do we call this a privilege?

BIBLE STUDY

1. Read Matt. 25:31-46 and point out (1) the names given to the principal person in the story; (2) in what surroundings He appears; (3) who will meet before His throne; (4) the groups into which He will divide them; (5) what He says to the group on His right hand; (6) to those on the left hand; (7) the final result.
2. In your opinion, why does Christ stress works of charity as He does in this story?

81

CHAPTER TWENTY

The Third Article --
of Sanctification

I believe in the Holy Ghost; the holy Christian Church, the Communion of Saints; the Forgiveness of sins; the Resurrection of the body; and the Life everlasting. Amen.

What does this mean?

Answer: I believe that I cannot by my own reason or strength believe in Jesus Christ my Lord, or come to Him;

but the Holy Ghost has called me through the gospel, enlightened me with His gifts, and sanctified and preserved me in the true faith;

in like manner as He calls, gathers, enlightens, and sanctifies the whole Christian Church on earth, and preserves it in union with Jesus Christ in the one true faith;

in which Christian Church He daily forgives abundantly all my sins, and the sins of all believers,

and at the last day will raise up me and all the dead, and will grant everlasting life to me and to all who believe in Christ. This is most certainly true.

In the Third Article I confess my faith in the Holy Spirit.

1. THE HOLY SPIRIT

The Bible speaks of the Spirit of God and the spirit of man. The word "spirit" is used in both cases.

From the very first, experience taught man the difference between his body and his spirit. Within his body was a power that he could neither see nor describe. His existence depended upon the presence of this power. He called it spirit. It was more powerful than his body, for without the spirit the body was dead. To man, spirit, soul, and life came to mean practically the same.

Since God in His work to reveal Himself is dependent upon human language, He used the word "Spirit" of Himself in order to make man realize that He is the creator of our spirits and the giver of all life. Though man's spirit is similar to God's Spirit, there is the same difference as there is between the creature and the creator.

The Spirit of God, the Holy Spirit, and the Holy Ghost are names for the same Person in the Godhead.

The Holy Spirit is true God together with the Father and the Son. He is the third person in the Trinity. (Chap. Twelve, 1.)

2. THE HOLY SPIRIT IS THE LIFE GIVER

Life in all its forms is created by the Holy Spirit.

When God created man, we are told:

And Jehovah God formed man of the dust of the ground, and breathed into his nostrils the breath of life; and man became a living soul (Gen. 2:7) .

The Holy Spirit also creates spiritual life, that is, trust in Jesus Christ and love and obedience to Him.

The love of God hath been shed abroad in our hearts through the Holy Spirit which was given unto us (Rom. 5:5) .

3. THE HOLY SPIRIT DECLARES CHRIST

Christ Himself made clear the relation between His work and the work of the Holy Spirit.

He shall glorify Me; for He shall take of Mine, and shall declare it unto you (John 16:14)

Christ revealed the Father, died for our sins, and won the victory over Satan, sin, and death. He made forgiveness of sin possible. It is by faith in Him that we are saved. For He alone is the Savior.

It is the work of the Holy Spirit through the means of grace, the Word and the Sacraments, to lead us to know Jesus Christ, to accept Him as our Savior and Lord, and to live in fellowship with Him. Therefore, Jesus said to His disciples:

"When the Comforter is come, whom I will send unto you from the Father, even the Spirit of truth, which proceedeth from the Father, He shall bear witness of Me" (John 15:26).

The Holy Spirit does not bring to man a new truth. Whether dealing with God or man, whether with the past, the present, or the future, He has no other material to work with, no other truth to teach than that which is found in Christ as told in the Bible.

4. THE HOLY SPIRIT LEADS ME TO CHRIST

"I believe that I cannot by my own reason or strength believe in Jesus Christ my Lord, or come to Him; but the Holy Ghost has called me through the Gospel, enlightened me with His gifts, and sanctified and preserved me in the true faith."

The natural man receiveth not the things of the Spirit of God, for they are foolishness unto him; and he cannot know them, because they are spiritually judged (I Cor. 2: 14).

The natural man is man in the darkness and with the corrupted nature brought upon him by sin (Chap. Fourteen, 1). Of himself he is neither able to grasp the truth in Christ nor willing to surrender himself to Christ.

No man can say, Jesus is Lord, but in the Holy Spirit (I Cor. 12:3).

Prayer:

> O Spirit blest, we Thee entreat:
> O grant us that we ever,
> With heart and soul, as it is meet,
> May serve our Lord and Savior
> And Him confess till our last breath,
> As Lord of life and Lord of death
> And give Him praise and honor. Amen.
>
> (L. H. No. 380, v. 2)

QUESTIONS

(To be answered in writing, except 1 and 2)

1. Look up and read in your Bible all Bible passages quoted in this chapter. Underscore them in your Bible.

2. Be ready to recite the material that is to be memorized.

3. Read on the Trinity in Chapter Twelve, 1, and state why you believe that the Holy Spirit is (1) a person, and (2) true God.

4. Why may the Holy Spirit be called "Life Giver"?

5. State to whom the Holy Spirit gives life.

6. Explain the relation between the work of Christ and the work of the Spirit.

7. By what means does the Holy Spirit lead us to faith in Christ?

8. Why does not the Spirit bring us a new revelation?

9. State why we cannot by our own reason and strength believe on Jesus or come to Him.

10. What is meant by "the natural man"?

11. Who alone can help us to say: "Jesus is Lord"?

12. Why is it so difficult to say: "Jesus is Lord"?

13. Do you in this chapter find anything of special importance for yourself?

BIBLE STUDY

The prophet Ezekiel worked among Israel in the Babylonian captivity.

After reading Ez. 37:1-14, point out (1) what the prophet saw; (2) what he was told to do; (3) what happened when he did as he was told; (4) what difference it would make if you in verse 9 read Spirit instead of wind (the Hebrew word can be translated both Spirit and wind); (5) who were these dry bones; (6) what Israel was saying; (7) what the prophet as a result of the vision should tell Israel (graves in verses 12 and 13 are symbolic for captivity); (8) in what way God was going to renew Israel.

CHAPTER TWENTY-ONE

The Third Article - -

THE HOLY CHRISTIAN CHURCH, THE COMMUNION OF SAINTS

"I believe in . . . the holy Christian Church, the Communion of Saints."

1. THE BIRTH OF THE CHRISTIAN CHURCH

Jesus had promised the disciples to send them the Holy Spirit. This promise was fulfilled on Pentecost Sunday.

Filled with the Holy Spirit, Peter preached the crucified and risen Jesus as Lord and Christ and told the people: "Repent ye, and be baptized every one of you in the name of Jesus Christ unto the remission of your sins" (Acts 2:38). "They then that received his word were baptized; and there were added unto them in that day about three thousand souls" (Acts 2:41).

Thus the Christian Church came into existence. Pentecost Sunday is the birthday of the church.

2. BUILT ON THE ROCK

The holy Christian Church is not built on any human foundation. Its foundation is Jesus Christ.

Once Christ asked the disciples: "Who say ye that I am?" Peter, as their spokesman, answered: "Thou art the Christ, the Son of the living God." Then Jesus said:

Upon this rock I will build My Church (Matt. 16:18).

Christ did not build His Church upon the man, but upon the truth confessed by Peter, that Jesus is the Son of the living God. Christ Jesus is the "Rock of Ages."

86

3. MEMBERSHIP

Who are members of the holy Christian Church? Only God's children are members. It is the Holy Spirit and not the vote of the congregation that inscribes a person on the records of God's church. He made me a member when I was baptized. He brought me into fellowship with Jesus Christ and added me to the holy Christian Church.

The Lord added to them day by day those that were saved (Acts 2:47).

This membership may be lost. If I turn away from Christ and do not trust and love Him but love and serve sin, then I am no longer a child of God and no longer a member of His church. If this should be the case, God calls upon me to confess my sin to Him and accept His forgiveness that He may restore my membership.

4. THE COMMUNION OF SAINTS

This is another name for the Christian Church. The members are saints. The word "saints" does not refer to the "St." placed before the names of certain persons long ago dead, e.g., St. Thomas and St. Ann. Whether they all belonged to the communion of saints, only God knows. "Saints" in the Third Article include God's children and no one else. God made them saints when He gave them the Holy Spirit to dwell in them. They have fellowship with Jesus Christ and with one another.

Our fellowship is with the Father and with His Son Jesus Christ (I John 1:3).

We know we have passed out of death into life, because we love the brethren (I John 3:14).

The love God's children have for one another forms a tie stronger than any other fellowship. The proud Pharisee Paul hated and persecuted the Christians. As soon as he became a Christian himself, he gave his life in the service of Christ and His people, whether Jews or Gentiles.

5. THE PRIESTHOOD OF BELIEVERS

The Holy Spirit calls the believers to serve as priests before God and men.

Ye also . . . are . . . to be a holy priesthood, to offer up spiritual sacrifices, acceptable to God through Jesus Christ (I Peter 2:5). Every believer has the privilege of bringing his sacrifices of prayer, praise and thanksgiving directly to God without any other middleman than Jesus Christ.

Believers are also called to be witnesses for Christ. In fact, His work cannot be done without this witnessing.

Ye are . . . a royal priesthood . . . that ye may show forth the excellencies of Him who called you out of darkness into His marvelous light (I Peter 2:9).

6. THE MARKS OF THE HOLY CHRISTIAN CHURCH

The church as the communion of saints is (I) holy, (II) one, (III) victorious, and (IV) perpetual.

I. The Christian Church is holy. It is the Holy Spirit that makes the church holy. The Holy Spirit dwells in the church because He dwells in its members, the saints.

II. The Christian Church is one. Using human illustrations, the apostle calls the church the body of Christ. The body is one body, though it has many members.

In one Spirit were we all baptized into one body, whether Jews or Greeks, whether bond or free (I Cor. 12:13).

So completely does the Holy Spirit change a person when he becomes a child of God, that the rich and the poor, the learned and the ignorant, the colored and the white, are united in one body in Christ.

Some church bodies use the word catholic instead of Christian. They read: I believe . . . in the holy catholic church. Catholic is then used in its original sense, meaning universal.

III. The Christian Church is victorious. This does not mean that the church ever shall become the ruler over the world and its kingdoms. Such dreams have no support in the Word of God. The church is not a political, financial, or military power. That the church is victorious means that Jesus Christ will keep and guard all believers, give them victory over sin, death, and the power of the devil, and gather them one by one into the church triumphant.

The gates of Hades shall not prevail against it (Matt. 16:18).

IV. The Christian Church is perpetual. Individuals die and church organizations change and even disappear, but the communion of saints will go on for ever. The Holy

Spirit, through the means of grace, will continue His work to call, gather, enlighten, and sanctify souls in Christ Jesus, and preserve them in the true faith.

Prayer:

> Oh, make Thy Church, dear Savior,
> A lamp of burnished gold,
> To bear before the nations
> Thy true light as of old;
> Oh, teach Thy wandering pilgrims
> By this their path to trace,
> Till, clouds and darkness ended,
> They see Thee face to face. Amen.

(L. H. No. 134, v. 4)

WORD STUDY

Communion: fellowship.

QUESTIONS
(To be answered in writing, except 1 and 2)

1. Look up and read in your Bible the Bible passages quoted in this chapter. Underscore them in your Bible
2. Be ready to recite the material that is to be memorized.
3. When was the Christian Church born?
4. What did Peter preach that day?
5. What did he urge the people to do?
6. Explain what Christ meant by the rock upon which He would build His church.
7. How do we become members of the holy Christian Church?
8. Who are members of the holy Christian Church?
9. What is the Communion of Saints?
10. Who are these saints?
11. How did they become saints?
12. With whom do they have communion?
13. How close is this communion?
14. Who belongs to the priesthood of believers?
15. What is their work as priests?
16. How can the Christian Church be holy?
17. State the reason why there is only one Christian Church.
18. In what way is the Christian Church victorious?
19. Point out how the church is perpetual.
20. Of what value is the holy Christian Church to you?

BIBLE STUDY

After reading Eph. 4:1-6, point out (1) why Paul calls himself the prisoner in the Lord (see Acts 28:16); (2) what he entreats them to do; (3) the kind of calling he refers to in v. 1; (4) the things to which they should pay special attention (make a list of them); (5) the meaning of the "unity of the Spirit"; (6) the reason for keeping the unity of the Spirit (verses 4-6).

CHAPTER TWENTY-TWO

The Third Article--

THE ORGANIZED CHURCH

The holy Christian Church of the Third Article is the communion of saints. It is also called the congregation of saints. It is this church that is holy, one, victorious, and perpetual. It is to this church that Christ entrusted the means of grace.

The Augsburg Confession says: "The church is the congregation of saints, in which the gospel is rightly taught and the Sacraments are rightly administered."

In the congregation of saints there is no distinction of rank or class. "Be not ye called Rabbi; for one is your teacher, and all ye are brethren. And call no man your father on the earth; for one is your father, even He who is in heaven. Neither be ye called master; for one is your master, even the Christ" (Matt. 23:8-10).

1. CHRIST GAVE HIS CHURCH WORK TO DO

"Go, and make all nations disciples," was the command Jesus gave His disciples. Some of this work each believer could do alone. He could pray, be a witness for Christ in his daily life, instruct his own children, and help the needy that came to him. Other parts of the work he could not do without the help of other believers. He could not educate pastors, missionaries, and teachers, and support them. He could not build churches and maintain them, establish schools and finance them. Such work could be done only by a group of believers banding themselves together for this purpose. So organization became a necessity.

2. THE CHURCH IS ORGANIZED

At first the apostles were the leaders of the church. However, as the church grew and the work increased, they needed help. The church at Jerusalem elected seven deacons to take care of the poor. When a group of people were converted in a place, presbyters or elders were chosen from the group and placed in charge of the local work. These elders were also called bishops or overseers. They were the pastors of the congregations. There were, besides, deacons and deaconesses, evangelists, teachers, prophets and other workers, some called directly by God, others elected by the congregation.

At first, the different congregations were bound together by no synodical organization. The bond between them was their faith in Jesus Christ and their brotherly love.

Later, one of the elders or bishops in a larger city became the overseer over the congregations and their elders in the neighborhood, and the title bishop was then used only of these overseers. Still later, the bishops in Jerusalem, Antioch, Alexandria, Constantinople, and Rome assumed authority over the bishops in their territory and were called metropolitans. Finally, the bishop or metropolitan at Rome claimed authority over the whole Christian Church and was called pope, from the Latin papa which means father. He claimed to be Christ's representative on earth. This church became known as the Roman Catholic Church.

3. THE MEMBERSHIP CHANGES

The persecutions of the Christians, during the first three centuries after Christ, served quite effectively to keep hypocrites from joining the church. When the emperor Constantine in the fourth century declared the Christian religion to be the religion of the empire, the situation changed. Many joined the church in order to gain favor with the emperor. Others joined because it helped business or gave social standing. The result was that people who knew neither conversion nor the true faith in Christ far outnumbered the true believers in the church. More and more they became the rulers of the church organization.

4. FALSE TEACHINGS CREEP IN

One of the results of the change in membership was an increasing number of false teachings.

The pastor became a priest. A priest is a mediator between God and man. He had the power to repeat Christ's sacrifice on the cross for man's sins. Only the priest should drink the wine at the Lord's Supper. The priests were forbidden to marry. Purgatory was invented. Here the departed Catholics through sufferings paid for their sins and were made ready for heaven. All non-Catholics were condemned. They were not allowed even in purgatory. The Bible must be understood in harmony with the traditions of the church. The saints did more good works than they needed. This sum of additional good works was in the possession of the church, that is of the pope. He could use these extra works for the benefit of those who had too little. This was called indulgence or remission of punishment not already forgiven. Sale of indulgence developed into big business. The saints, that is, those whom the Catholic Church declared to be saints, had the power to intercede for man with God. These and many other teachings contrary to God's Word were adopted by the church.

A church ritual was built up in harmony with the false teachings. Additions or changes in the ritual always increased the prominence and power of the priests. Titles were invented, the one more imposing than the other. Gowns became more and more brilliant as the priest advanced to higher positions.

5. THE LUTHERAN CHURCH APPEARS

When Martin Luther came to realize that the Roman Catholic Church both taught and practiced contrary to God's Word, he spoke and wrote against the false teachings and practices. He thought that the pope would be anxious to reform the church as soon as he saw how sorely it was needed. Instead, the pope condemned Luther and expelled him from the church. As a result Luther and his followers were forced to establish themselves outside of the Roman Catholic Church. Those that followed Luther called themselves the Evangelicals, but later the name Lutheran was used.

6. WHAT THE LUTHERAN CHURCH CONFESSES

The Lutheran Church went back to the teachings of God's Word. It is therefore not a new church, but the apostolic church restored. The Lutherans accept the three ancient confessions, the Apostolic Creed, the Nicene Creed, and the Athanasian Creed.[1] Besides, they accept Luther's Small Catechism and the Augsburg Confession as their particular creeds. The Lutheran Church is spoken of as the church of the Augsburg Confession.

7. WHAT THE LUTHERAN CHURCH TEACHES

The book we are now studying presents the Lutheran faith. Here we give only a summary of our special teachings.

The Bible is God's Word. It is the only authority in all things concerning our salvation. The church and all its activities are subject to and judged by God's Word. Jesus Christ is the only mediator between God and man. Man is saved by faith in Jesus Christ. True faith is active in good works. We do not pray to the saints. Even the saints were sinners, lacking the perfection God's law demands. They were saved by grace alone. At death all true believers go home to God. The holy Christian Church consists of all true believers in Christ. It is to them that the means of grace have been entrusted. The pope is not Christ's representative on earth. Unless he is a child of God, the pope does not even belong to the holy Christian Church. All believers are priests before God. The pastor is a shepherd of souls, a preacher, and a teacher. His main function is to preach the gospel. He is not a priest. In Baptism the Holy Spirit creates a new spiritual life. At the Lord's Supper both bread and wine are given to the communicants. In and with the bread and wine Christ gives His body and blood. The pastor does not repeat the sacrifice of Christ. The main purpose of the church services is the preaching of the gospel, including the administration of the Sacraments.

---

[1] The Nicene Creed was adopted in 325 A. D. at Nicæa in Asia Minor. It stresses the divinity of Christ. The Athanasian Creed was composed most likely in Southern France between 450 and 600 A. D. It deals especially with the Trinity of God. The Augsburg Confession was read at the diet at Augsburg, Germany, in 1530. It sets forth the Lutheran teachings and practices.

8. THE LOCAL CONGREGATION

The local congregation is the organized church in a locality. As is always the case in the organized church, hypocrites are found in the local congregation. The congregation is the highest authority in its own affairs. Still, it cannot do as it pleases. God's Word is the authority over the congregation. If the congregation disobeys the Word, it sins.

In order to do the work that the single congregation cannot do, several congregations, my own included, form a synod. It is the synod that manages the education of pastors, missionaries, teachers, and deaconesses, directs home and foreign missions, supervises inner mission (charity) work, and is in charge of the work the congregations have undertaken as a common task. The synod and its officers have no other authority than the authority given them by the congregations.

9. PRIVILEGES AND RESPONSIBILITIES

It is a privilege to belong to the Christian Church even though its organized form has many shortcomings. Every one needs the means of grace, and it is the church that has these means. And Christian fellowship is found only in the Christian Church.

The local congregation, as well as the synod, has a large responsibility for the work Christ gave His followers to do. Each member shares this responsibility. Only careless and selfish members will fail to pray for their congregation and synod. A true member will not only pray, but gladly take his share of the work and liberally contribute in money and service to the local and synodical work. (Chap. Nine, 7.)

A true member will also watch and help to guard his congregation and synod against false teachings, ungodly practices, and anything that will destroy the spiritual life and work of his church.

The church should have the warmest love of every member.

Prayer:

I thank Thee, Lord Jesus, for my congregation and for the privilege of being a member of Thy church. Send Thy Holy Spirit and purify Thy church on earth and make it a true witness of Thee. Forgive our sins and glorify Thy name. Amen.

WORD STUDY
Ritual: ceremonies. Hypocrite: one who pretends, a cheat.

QUESTIONS
(To be answered in writing, except 1)

1. Be ready to recite the three Articles of Faith.
2. What is meant by the holy Christian Church in the Third Article?
3. State the definition of the church given by the Augsburg Confession.
4. Point out the work Christ gave His church to do.
5. Why was it necessary to organize the church?
6. Describe the growth of organization in the early church.
7. What effect did the persecutions have upon the membership of the church?
8. How did the character of the membership change?
9. How did the change of membership affect the teachings of the church?
10. Why did the Lutheran Church become a separate church?
11. Name the Confessions of the Lutheran Church.
12. Point out differences between Lutheran teachings and those of the Roman Catholic Church.
13. What authority has the local congregation?
14. Name the authority over the congregation.
15. Why do congregations unite in synods?
16. What authority has the synod and its officers?
17. Why is it a privilege to belong to a Christian congregation?
18. State your responsibilities to your congregation.

BIBLE STUDY
Read Tit. 1:5-9 and (1) state what Titus should do in Crete; (2) make a list of the qualifications required in an elder; (3) explain why elder and bishop must be the same person; (4) point out the work of the elder (last part of v. 9)

Who is doing the work of an elder in your congregation?

CHAPTER TWENTY-THREE

The Third Article - -

THE FORGIVENESS OF SIN

"In which Christian Church He daily forgives abundantly all my sins, and the sins of all believers."

1. I NEED FORGIVENESS OF SIN

In my relation to God sin comes in as a serious matter. God is holy, and His law is holy, and I have broken His law. How can I meet Him? Neither tears nor promises nor work can undo the wrong I have done. "Though thou wash thee with lye, and take thee much soap, yet thine iniquity is marked before Me, saith the Lord Jehovah" (Jer. 2:22).

Even though I am a child of God, still I find much sin in myself. How often I have been filled with worry instead of trust in my heavenly Father. How often my heart is cold toward Him and disobedient and rebellious. I still find much impurity in this heart of mine. Often I find myself slow, unwilling, and joyless in His service. How careless I have been many a time in my prayer life. And how many honest promises to Him have I not broken.

What hope of salvation is there for such a one?

Without the forgiveness of sins there would be no hope.

2. FORGIVENESS OF SINS PROVIDED BY CHRIST

Forgiveness of sins was the purpose and aim of Christ's suffering and death. By raising Christ from the dead and setting Him at His right hand, God bound Himself to for-

96

give sins. Therefore, the apostle John says: *If we confess our sins, He is faithful and righteous to forgive us our sins, and to cleanse us from all unrighteousness* (I John 1:9).

When I confess my sins to God and ask forgiveness, He would be neither faithful nor righteous if He refused to forgive. He would then require two deaths for my sins, Christ's and mine. The holy God could do no such thing.

In Christ we have our redemption, the forgiveness of our sins (Col. 1:14).

3. DAILY FORGIVENESS OF SINS

"In which Christian Church He daily forgives abundantly all my sins and the sins of all believers."

Daily does not mean once a day. It means all the time every day. I need forgiveness all the time. Not for a minute do I in this life reach perfection in trust, love, and obedience to my Lord. *Not that I have already obtained, or am already made perfect; but I press on* (Phil. 3:12).

A child of God is painfully aware of his imperfection. It grieves him. Again and again he must speak to his heavenly Father about it and ask His forgiveness. Otherwise he will have no peace in his conscience. What gives him peace is that God forgives his sins all the time.

Justified by faith we have peace with God through our Lord Jesus Christ (Rom. 5:1).

4. ABUNDANT FORGIVENESS OF SINS

"He daily forgives abundantly all my sins."

I have an abundance of sin. It overflows. It is not the outward acts alone that bring this confession. Too often they are not what they should be. Still, the evil that clings to me in my thoughts and desires is even more serious. Often I find this inward evil at work when the outward act is blameless. To all this I have to add my imperfect trust, love, and obedience to my Savior. Yes, my sin is abundant.

Still, God's forgiveness is more abundant. It is so plentiful that it blots out every sin that I confess to Him. With God there is plentiful forgiveness for the greatest sin.

Come now, and let us reason together, saith the Lord; though your sins be as scarlet, they shall be as white as snow;

though they be red like crimson, they shall be as wool (Is. 1:18).

Where sin abounded, grace did abound more exceedingly (Rom. 5:20).

5. FORGIVENESS OF SINS TO ALL BELIEVERS

"He daily forgives abundantly . . . the sins of all believers."

God offers forgiveness of sins to all, but only the believers accept it. As a result, only their sins are forgiven. It is by believing, trusting God's word about the forgiveness of my sins for Christ's sake, that I accept what He offers. Then God's forgiveness is mine. I can rest in it and rejoice.

6. FORGIVENESS OF SINS THROUGH THE MEANS OF GRACE

God forgives my sins through the means of grace, that is, through the Word and the Sacraments.

The means of grace may be compared to the pipes that bring the water into the house. The pipes are not the source of the water supply. Neither are the means of grace the source of the forgiveness of sins. God is the source. As the water flows through the pipes so the forgiveness of sins flows from God through the means of grace.

7. JUSTIFICATION BY FAITH

In the language of the church, forgiveness of sins is called justification by faith.

Every one that believes in Jesus Christ is declared righteous by God. His sins are blotted out and he is clothed in the righteousness of Christ. God takes away the sin that the sinner has and gives him the righteousness that Christ has. God looks upon the believer as though he had never sinned.

A man is not justified by the works of the law but through faith in Jesus Christ (Gal. 2:16).

A definition: Justification by faith is an act of God by which He declares that person just and righteous who believes in Jesus Christ as his Savior and Lord

It was this teaching that was the real cause for the pope's condemnation of Luther. Justification by faith alone is rejected by the Roman Catholic Church.

98

Prayer:

Just as I am, without one plea,
But that Thy blood was shed for me,
And that Thou bidst me come to Thee,
O Lamb of God, I come, I come.

Just as I am, and waiting not
To rid myself of one dark blot,
To Thee, whose blood can cleanse each spot,
O Lamb of God, I come, I come.

Just as I am! Thou wilt receive,
Wilt welcome, pardon, cleanse, relieve;
Because Thy promise I believe,
O Lamb of God, I come, I come. Amen.

(L. H. No. 447, vv. 1, 2, and 5)

QUESTIONS

(To be answered in writing, except 1 and 2)

1. Look up and read in your Bible the Bible passages quoted in this chapter. Underscore them in your Bible.
2. Be ready to recite the material that is to be memorized.
3. State the reason why I cannot wash away my sins.
4. Point out sins that a child of God finds in himself.
5. How is God faithful and righteous when He forgives sins?
6. State the meaning of "daily."
7. Why does a child of God need daily forgiveness?
8. How abundant is God's forgiveness of sins?
9. Why do only believers receive forgiveness of sins?
10. What is meant by a believer?
11. Why may the means of grace be likened to water pipes?
12. Give the reason why there is no forgiveness of sins apart from the means of grace.
13. When God justifies a sinner, what does He take away and what does He give?
14. Explain justification by faith.
15. In what ways has this lesson been of help to you?

BIBLE STUDY

After reading Zech. 3:1-5 point out (1) where the high-priest was standing; (2) what you think Satan was doing (Satan means adversary); (3) why the Lord rebuked Satan; (4) what the Lord meant when He said that Joshua was a brand plucked out of the fire; (5) how Joshua was clothed; (6) what his clothing signified; (7) what the Lord commanded be taken from Joshua; (8) what this act signified; (9) what kind of clothes were put on him; (10) how this story illustrates justification by faith.

99

CHAPTER TWENTY-FOUR

The Third Article - -

THE HOLY SPIRIT CALLS AND ENLIGHTENS ME

It is the work of the Holy Spirit to convince me that I need forgiveness of sins. It is also His work to lead me to accept forgiveness and to believe in Jesus Christ all the days of my life.

In the study of the Holy Spirit's work in the heart we will follow the order given in the Catechism: "The Holy Ghost has called me through the gospel, enlightened me with His gifts, and sanctified and preserved me in the true faith."

1. THE HOLY SPIRIT CALLS ME

"I believe that the Holy Ghost has called me through the gospel."

The gospel invites me to come to Jesus Christ with my sins, that He may forgive them. Through the church this invitation came to me when I was a little child. In response to that invitation I was baptized. Then God forgave my sins, and I became His child.

As I grew from year to year and was instructed in the Word of God, I realized that I failed to be the obedient, God-loving child that I ought to be. There were small sins and big sins and the conscience accused me. "Thou gavest also Thy good Spirit to instruct them" (Neh. 9:20).

Throughout these years the Holy Spirit constantly renewed the gospel call, the invitation to tell God about my sins and receive the forgiveness that Christ had won for me.

At times I have been unwilling to accept the invitation. When I was angry with someone and planned to return evil for evil, I did not like to tell God about it. I wanted my revenge. But I was not happy.

But the Holy Spirit did not fail me. He worked in my conscience through the law of God to convince me of the wrong I was doing. He urged and urged me to repent of my sin.

And all the time the Holy Spirit was repeating the gospel invitation to come and confess my sin to God that it might be blotted out in the blood of Christ. When I confessed and accepted God's forgiveness, I found peace.

I acknowledged my sin unto Thee, and mine iniquity did I not hide; I said, I will confess my transgressions unto the Lord; and Thou forgavest the iniquity of my sin (Ps. 32:5).

2. REPENTANCE

We have already mentioned repentance. Before going farther we must learn more about this experience.

When the Word of God says, "Repent," it means that I should honestly admit that I have done wrong and show my sorrow by seeking God's forgiveness and by turning away from the road of sin.

This sorrow does not make God more willing to forgive sin, but it makes me willing to accept God's forgiveness and let God save me from the power sin has over me. Repentance is therefore necessary if I shall be saved.

Except ye repent, ye shall all in like manner perish (Luke 13:3).

The sorrow may be more or less painful. The proof of its genuineness is that I begin to hate my sin and honestly turn to God to be saved from it.

The fear of the Lord is to hate evil (Prov. 8:13).

Godly sorrow worketh repentance unto salvation, a repentance which bringeth no regret (II Cor. 7:10).

It is evident that a Christian will experience such sorrow throughout his whole life. Again and again the Holy Spirit will point out shortcomings, failures, and sins that will fill him with grief over the fact that he still is so little like his Savior and Friend.

A Christian will, therefore, experience daily repentance.

3. DESTROYING THE CONSCIENCE

A man may go on refusing to heed the Holy Spirit's call to repentance. If he does, he will ruin his conscience. We then say that the conscience is hardened.

The refusal may be deliberate, as in the case of Judas. The repeated warnings of Jesus only made him harder. The overwhelming majority of the people of Israel in Old Testament times acted in the same way. God said of them:

I have spread out My hands all the day unto a rebellious people, that walk in a way that is not good, after their own thoughts (Is. 65:2).

It is with sorrow we admit that there are such people even in our own congregations.

Then there are those who take their relation to God more seriously, but who have some pet sins they do not want to give up. Ananias and Sapphira were of that type (Acts 5: 1-11). Their pet sin was love of money. They would not give up the sin they loved and enjoyed

No man can serve two masters. . . . Ye cannot serve God and mammon (Matt. 6:24).

Young friends, let us give ourselves whole-heartedly to Christ. Only then can He give us the joy of His salvation.

4. THE HOLY SPIRIT ENLIGHTENS

"I believe that the Holy Ghost has . . . enlightened me with His gifts."

It is not enough that the Holy Spirit calls me. He must also enlighten me. I need a great deal of light. The gifts He uses in this work are the law and the gospel.

I. The Holy Spirit enlightens me to see that I am a lost sinner. By nature I am not willing to admit that I am a lost and condemned sinner. Excusing my weaknesses, I like to think of myself as a pretty good person, at least as good as my neighbor and generally a little better. I admit, of course, that I need some forgiveness, but a little forgiveness God will not deny me, and so my situation is rather hopeful.

It is the Holy Spirit that clears up the confused thinking and the equally confused conscience. He makes me face God's law in my daily life. I learn to judge myself by what God says. The result is a clearer understanding of God's holy will as well as a growing knowledge of my own sinfulness.

In the case of a baptized child who is instructed in the way of salvation and who continues to trust and serve the Lord, the realization of his sinfulness grows from year to year. When he becomes an older and more experienced Christian, he will know a great deal more about his sinfulness than when he was a confirmand.

One who has been baptized and instructed, but who has strayed away from God, may come to a more sudden realization of his lost condition. Still, this is only the beginning. He, too, needs more and more light. In the school of daily living, the Holy Spirit must teach him the lesson that in himself he is but a lost and condemned creature.

II. The Holy Spirit enlightens me to see Jesus as my Savior. This is an experience common to all God's children. Still, it cannot be fully explained. To grasp the truth with our mind is not the same as to experience the truth. Without experiencing the saving truth we know no more about it than we know of a person by putting on his cover-all.

This work of the Holy Spirit may be stated as follows: When the good tidings of Jesus Christ come to me as I read or hear or remember the gospel, the Holy Spirit leads me to see that Christ died for *me*, that His blood blots out all *my* transgressions, that all *my* sins are now forgiven, and that I am saved. He makes Christ so real, so great to me that I see myself saved in Him.

This work the Holy Spirit must continue every day as long as I live. By my own reason or strength I am no more able to believe in Christ today than yesterday. Left to myself, I would lose Christ and the forgiveness of my sins.

Prayer:

> Gracious Spirit, Dove divine!
> Let Thy light within me shine;
> All my guilty fears remove,
> Fill me with Thy heavenly love.

Speak Thy pardoning grace to me,
Set the burdened sinner free;
Lead me to the Lamb of God;
Wash me in His precious blood. Amen.

(L. H., No. 376, vv. 1 and 2)

WORD STUDY

Enlighten: make one see what he otherwise does not see.

QUESTIONS

(To be answered in writing, except 1 and 2)

1. Look up and read in your Bible the Bible passages quoted in this chapter. Underscore them in your Bible.
2. Be ready to recite the material that is to be memorized.
3. What is the gospel call?
4. When did the gospel call first come to me?
5. Why have I at times refused to heed the gospel call?
6. Describe the experience when I refused to heed the gospel call.
7. What happened when I admitted my sin and confessed it to God?
8. What is repentance?
9. Why is repentance necessary?
10. State the effect of sorrow for my sin.
11. How much sorrow is necessary?
12. Why is daily repentance necessary?
13. Who hardens his conscience?
14. Point out the effects of hardening the conscience.
15. What do we mean when we say that the Holy Spirit enlightens?
16. How does the Holy Spirit enlighten me to see my sin?
17. Why does a baptized child need to be enlightened more and more with regard to its sin?
18. How does the Holy Spirit enlighten me to see Jesus as my Savior?
19. State how long this work must continue.
20. Why is an understanding of this work not enough?

BIBLE STUDY

After reading Ps. 32 point out (1) who is blessed; (2) the meaning of "the Lord imputeth not iniquity"; (3) why these words are added: "In whose spirit there is no guile"; (4) when David kept silence; (5) the effect of the silence; (6) why he suffered during his silence; (7) the meaning of "I acknowledged my sin"; (8) to whom he acknowledged it; (9) what happened when he confessed his sin.

CHAPTER TWENTY-FIVE

The Third Article --

FAITH AND REGENERATION

When the Holy Spirit enlightens me through the gospel, He produces three results: forgiveness of sin, faith, and a new life or regeneration.

These are three sides of the same act of the Holy Spirit. They take place at one and the same time. I cannot have forgiveness of sins without faith and without new life. Nor can I have new life without faith and forgiveness of sins.

It is impossible for us to understand all this. But let us remember that when we trust and obey the Word of God, the Holy Spirit will do His work in our souls, whether we understand much or little of it.

SAVING FAITH

When I speak of saving faith, the first question is, In whom do I believe? A drowning man may believe strongly in a person on shore, but that will not save him unless the person is able and willing to come to his rescue.

Saving faith is faith in the person Jesus Christ. He is both able and willing to save.

Believe on the Lord Jesus, and thou shalt be saved (Acts 16:31).

1. WHAT I BELIEVE ABOUT JESUS CHRIST

The next question is, What do I believe about Jesus Christ? Is He only the great teacher and example, the ideal man? Or is He the God-man who suffered and died for my sins?

"I believe that Jesus Christ, true God . . . and also true man, is my Lord, who has redeemed me . . . not with silver and gold, but with His holy and precious blood, and with His innocent sufferings and death; in order that I might be His own, live under Him in His kingdom, and serve Him in everlasting righteousness, innocence, and blessedness; even as He is risen from the dead, and lives and reigns to all eternity. This is most certainly true."

This is what I believe. It is this Jesus Christ I trust to save me. "He is able to save to the uttermost them that draw near unto God through Him" (Heb. 7:25).

2. SOME PRACTICAL PROBLEMS

A few problems in connection with saving faith should be discussed.

I. Knowledge and faith. Knowledge and faith are not the same. Of course, I must have knowledge of Christ if I am to believe in Him. I can not believe in one of whom I know nothing.

Belief cometh of hearing, and hearing by the word of Christ (Rom. 10:17).

Still, I may know all that the Bible tells of Christ and not have saving faith. I know with my intellect, my mind, I believe in Christ unto salvation with my heart, that is, with my whole personality. The heart includes intellect, will, and feelings. Everything in me is turned toward Christ. I rest in Christ and I want to live in Him.

With the heart man believeth unto righteousness (Rom. 10:10).

Saving faith, therefore, implies surrender and obedience to Christ.

II. Faith and feelings. Another difficulty is presented by my feelings. One day I feel happy and kindly disposed toward all people. It is easy to pray and I experience much blessing reading my Bible. Christ seems very near. On such a day there is no difficulty in believing the forgiveness of my sins and the love of Christ. I am sure I have saving faith.

106

The next day everything seems changed. I am out of sorts and rather impatient and dissatisfied. Prayer is an effort and joyless. Reading the Bible brings no comfort or strength. Christ seems far away and there is no feeling of peace in my soul. Then I have often thought that my faith must be a product of my imagination

Thank God, my salvation does not rest upon the loose and shifting sand of my feelings. Nor does my faith. Nowhere in His Word does God say, Feel and thou shalt be saved. It is in Christ I trust, and He does not change. "Jesus Christ is the same yesterday and today, yea and forever" (Heb. 13:8).

It is not my feelings that declare me righteous. It is God. And He declares me righteous, not because my feelings are pleasing and satisfactory, but because Christ died and rose for me and I take my refuge in Him, claim Him. Then I have a saving faith even when my conscience condemns me.

If our heart condemn us, God is greater than our heart, and knoweth all things (I John 3:20)

III. Weak and strong faith. My weak faith is one of my troubles. Too often I must say with the father of the epileptic boy:

I believe; help Thou my unbelief (Mark 9:24).

Like him I look partly at Jesus and partly at my own troubles. As a result, my faith wavers and becomes weak.

The centurion acted differently. He looked only at Jesus, and Jesus never failed and never would fail. So his faith was strong (Matt. 8:5-13).

In order that my faith may grow stronger, I must rely upon God's Word and upon nothing else. When I trust and depend upon His promises, He shall prove to me that He is trustworthy. Then my faith in God will grow.

A girl in a confirmation class was asked to explain faith. She answered: "I can not give a detailed explanation, but it seems to me that faith is to take God at His word."

3. SIN NOT TO BELIEVE

It is sin not to believe in Jesus Christ.

He that believeth not God hath made Him a liar; because he hath not believed in the witness that God hath borne concerning His Son (I John 5:10).

I can not commit the awful sin of making God a liar.

107

With my whole heart I confess: Lord Jesus, I believe that Thou art the Son of God, my Savior and my Lord.

REGENERATION

We come now to the work of the Holy Spirit which we call regeneration or the act of creating new life. We remember that the Spirit does not first create faith and then a new life. He creates both at the same time.

I. A new birth is necessary. The words of Jesus are very plain. *Verily, verily, I say unto thee, Except one be born anew, he cannot see the kingdom of God* (John 3:3).

The reason He gave is also plain.

That which is born of the flesh is flesh; and that which is born of the Spirit is spirit (John 3:6).

Flesh means sinful human nature. It is one of God's biological laws that sinful human nature produces sinful human nature.

The new life does not come out of man. Only the Holy Spirit has power to create new life. He creates this life, as He does all His saving work in the soul, through the means of grace.

II. The change. The change that takes place is described by God when He said to Israel: "A new heart also will I give you, and a new spirit will I put within you; and I will take away the stony heart out of your flesh, and I will give you a heart of flesh. And I will put My Spirit within you, and cause you to walk in My statutes" (Ez. 36:26-27).

The Holy Spirit enters the heart and makes it His dwelling place. He creates trust, love, and obedience to God, and peace in the conscience. This is the new life. The Spirit thus restores the image of God in part. It shall be restored fully when we enter eternal glory.

If any man is in Christ, he is a new creature; the old things are passed away; behold, they are become new (II Cor. 5:17).

Prayer:

> My faith looks up to Thee,
> Thou Lamb of Calvary,
> Savior divine!
> Now hear me while I pray,
> Take all my guilt away,
> Oh, let me from this day
> Be wholly Thine.

May Thy rich grace impart
Strength to my fainting heart,
My zeal inspire;
As Thou hast died for me,
O may my love to Thee
Pure, warm, and changeless be,
A living fire. Amen.

(L. H., No. 456, vv. 1 and 2)

QUESTIONS

(To be answered in writing, except 1 and 2)

1. Look up and read in your Bible the Bible passages quoted in this chapter. Underscore them in your Bible.
2. Be ready to recite the material that is to be memorized.
3. State the three results produced by the Holy Spirit when He enlightens a person.
4. What has Jesus Christ to do with saving faith?
5. What difference does it make whether I believe that Jesus is only a teacher and example or that He is the Son of God who died for my sins?
6. State the difference between knowledge of Jesus Christ and saving faith in Him.
7. What is the relation between saving faith and God's Word?
8. Why is it impossible to build saving faith on my feelings?
9. State what I must do when my heart condemns me
10. Point out reasons for weak faith.
11. What am I to do in order that my faith in God may grow stronger?
12. Why is it sin not to believe in Jesus Christ?
13. What does regeneration mean?
14. Why is regeneration necessary?
15. By what means does the Holy Spirit regenerate a sinner?
16. Point out the change wrought by the Holy Spirit in regeneration.
17. Name a person with whom Jesus had a conversation about regeneration.
18. In what ways has this chapter been of help to you?

BIBLE STUDY

After reading Matt. 15:21-28 point out (1) the location of Tyre and Sidon; (2) the nationality of the woman; (3) her trouble; (4) what made her think that Jesus could help her; (5) what she called Jesus; (6) why she cried (called loudly); (7) what she meant by "Have mercy on me"; (8) why Jesus did not answer her; (9) why the disciples wanted Him to send her away; (10) what He meant by His answer to them; (11) why the woman did not give up; (12) what Jesus answered her; (13) why she was not offended at this answer; (14) how her answer showed great faith; (15) the help she received.

CHAPTER TWENTY-SIX

The Third Article - -

THE HOLY SPIRIT SANCTIFIES AND PRESERVES

The word "Sanctification" in the sub-title to the Third Article includes all the work that the Holy Spirit does in my heart in order to make me a partaker of the salvation in Christ Jesus. In Luther's explanation, sanctification means the daily renewal. The Holy Spirit daily renews the believer's faith, love, and obedience, and makes him grow in Christ-likeness. He makes the believer fight the sins that seek to master him. This is sanctification.

SANCTIFICATION

"I believe that . . . the Holy Ghost has . . . sanctified and preserved me in the true faith." It is by sanctifying me in the true faith that the Holy Spirit preserves me in the true faith.

1. SANCTIFICATION NECESSARY

My spiritual life is under a heavy strain every day. I am facing temptations from within and from without. They must be overcome. I should love God above all things and my neighbor as myself. I should be pure in thoughts, truthful and kind in words, unselfish and manly in deeds. The strength needed, I have not in myself. At times the fight makes me tired and disheartened. Sinful lusts stir within. My heart grows cold, my prayers are without life or even neglected. Unless restored, there would soon be no saving faith, no true love, no willing obedience.

Only the Holy Spirit is able to restore my spiritual life. He alone can renew my faith and love and enable me to serve my Lord and Savior in a joyful spirit.

2. SANCTIFICATION A WORK OF GRACE

Grace is goodness I have not deserved. It is *grace* that God loves me. It is *grace* that He sent His Son to be my Savior and Lord. It is *grace* that He sent the Holy Spirit. It is *grace* that He established the church. It is *grace* that He gave the Word and the Sacraments. It is *grace* that He forgives my sins. It is *grace* that He calls, enlightens, sanctifies, and preserves me. It is *grace* that He glorifies me in His eternal home. My salvation from beginning to end is God's grace and God's gift.

By grace have ye been saved through faith; and that not of yourselves, it is the gift of God (Eph. 2:8).

3. SANCTIFICATION THROUGH THE MEANS OF GRACE

The Holy Spirit does all His work in my soul, from first to last, through the Word and the Sacraments. Apart from these means of grace there is no sanctification; as there is no call, no enlightening, no forgiveness of sins, no faith, no regeneration, no preservation, and no glorification.

The use of God's Word is necessary for my sanctification. Unless the Word is used, the new life will die from starvation. I must use it in my home and I must attend the services where God's Word is preached. I should also keep in mind God's covenant in my Baptism and the life to which I was then dedicated. And when confirmed, I should be a frequent guest at the Lord's Supper.

To this must be added prayer. Unless I open my heart to God in prayer, the Holy Spirit cannot do His work in me.

4. SANCTIFIED IN THE TRUE FAITH

I have the true faith when I trust in God's pure Word and live a holy life in accordance with its teachings. The Holy Spirit cannot sanctify me in the true faith if I believe false teachings. Neither can He sanctify me if I do not believe God's Word. Then I am dead spiritually, and He can-

111

not sanctify a dead man. It is the believer whom the Holy Spirit renews and makes to grow in Christ-likeness.

5. SANCTIFICATION AND OBEDIENCE

Without obedience to Christ I cannot live in fellowship with Him, much less grow in Christ-likeness. I do not grow merely by studying. I also grow by practicing, by doing. "Obedience is an organ of spiritual knowledge."

If ye abide in My word, then are ye truly My disciples; and ye shall know the truth, and the truth shall make you free (John 8:31-32).

I abide in Christ's word when I use it, trust it, and obey it.

6. SANCTIFICATION AND FORGIVENESS OF SINS

Sin, of which I am aware, brings an evil conscience, and I cannot serve God with an evil conscience. The Holy Spirit cannot renew my faith, love, and obedience so long as known sin stands between me and God. The sin must be removed and the conscience cleansed. Nothing but God's forgiveness can take away sin and bring peace to the conscience. There can be no sanctification without daily forgiveness of my sins.

In the light of such experiences the familiar words take on a new meaning: *"In which Christian Church He* (the Holy Spirit) *daily forgives abundantly all my sins, and the sins of all believers."*

7. THE SANCTIFIED LIFE

There are two natures in every child of God. The new nature, the new "I," is born of the Spirit, loves God, and wants to do His will. The Bible calls it the new man which we are urged to put on.

Put on the new man, that is being renewed unto knowledge after the image of Him that created him (Col. 3:10).

The old nature, the old "I," loves sin and wants to serve it. This old nature cannot be sanctified and only on the surface can it be civilized. Its life is to satisfy its desires. The Bible says the only solution is to destroy it.

Put to death, therefore, your members which are upon the earth: fornication, uncleanness, passion, evil desire, and covetousness, which is idolatry (Col. 3:5).

The road seems gloomy and joyless to those who have not entered upon it. To God's children it is a glorious road, though many a battle must be fought. The devil, the world, and our own flesh are always with us and cause difficulties and spiritual sufferings. Yet, all Christ's disciples testify that on this road Christ reveals His glory and the soul tastes and sees that the Lord is good. Here spiritual manhood grows. It is the road to victory over sin and self, the road of eternal life.

With good cheer I will trust and follow my Lord and Savior and press on fighting the good fight.

Being confident of this very thing, that He who began a good work in you will perfect it until the day of Jesus Christ (Phil. 1:6) .

THE RESURRECTION OF THE BODY

"I believe that . . . the Holy Ghost . . . at the last day will raise up me and all the dead."

The hour cometh, in which all that are in the tombs shall hear His voice, and shall come forth; they that have done good, unto the resurrection of life; and they that have done evil, unto the resurrection of judgment (John 5:28-29) .

On judgment day the voice of Christ shall be heard calling the dead to rise again. It is by the power of the life giving Holy Spirit that the dead bodies shall be brought back to life. Body and soul shall then be united. The body of God's children shall be glorified like the body of the risen Christ.

Jesus Christ shall fashion anew the body of our humiliation, that it may be conformed to the body of His glory (Phil. 3:21) .

LIFE EVERLASTING

"I believe that . . . the Holy Ghost . . . will grant everlasting life to me and to all who believe in Christ."

Life everlasting—that is the glory at the end of the earthly trail for God's people. Then shall I be like God for I shall see Him as He is (I John 3:2) . No more shall sin and evil plague me. "God shall wipe away every tear from their eyes; and death shall be no more; neither shall there be mourning, nor crying, nor pain, any more" (Rev. 21:4) . All the mental and spiritual powers, given me by God, shall then be unfolded into full use. This new experience shall swell the gratitude for all God's goodness into an eternal song of praise. And I shall always be with the Lord (I Thess. 4:17).

Blessed are the dead who die in the Lord from henceforth (Rev. 14:13).

And the others? It is a dreadful truth that those who do not accept Jesus Christ as their Savior shall suffer eternal punishment for their sins. We are unable to understand these deep things of God. We believe the words Jesus spoke: "Depart from Me, ye cursed, into the eternal fire which is prepared for the devil and his angels."

Such is my faith, founded on God's Word. I am grateful that I have been instructed in the truth that makes me wise unto salvation. I could not do without it. God grant that the truth I know in my head may be the language of my heart so that I really and truly believe in God the Father, Son, and Holy Spirit.

* * *

We have now finished the second lesson in our study of God's way of salvation. The Ten Commandments taught us the first lesson. By instructing us how God's children should live, the Commandments convicted us of being lost and condemned sinners. The Creed teaches us the second lesson. God, our heavenly Father, so loved the world that He gave His Son Jesus Christ to die for our sins. Through the means of grace the Holy Spirit points us to Him. "Believe on the Lord Jesus, and thou shalt be saved."

Prayer:

> Jesus, Jesus, only Jesus,
> Can my heartfelt longing still;
> See, I pledge myself to Jesus,
> What He wills, alone to will.
> For my heart, which He hath filled,
> Ever cries: Lord, as Thou wilt.
>
> Lord, my praise shall be unceasing,
> For Thou gav'st Thyself to me,
> And besides so many a blessing
> That I now sing joyfully:
> Be it unto me, my shield,
> As Thou wilt, Lord, as Thou wilt. Amen.
>
> (L. H. No. 353, vv. 1 and 5)

114

QUESTIONS

(To be answered in writing, except 1 and 2)

1. Look up and read in your Bible the Bible passages quoted in this chapter. Underscore them in your Bible.
2. Be ready to recite the material that is to be memorized.
3. How is the word "sanctification" used in the sub-title to the Third Article?
4. What is its meaning as used by Luther in the explanation to the article?
5. State the reason why sanctification is necessary.
6. Point out what it is that must be renewed daily.
7. What is grace?
8. To what extent am I saved by grace?
9. To what extent does the Holy Spirit use the means of grace in His work to save man?
10. Why is prayer necessary if the Holy Spirit shall renew my spiritual life?
11. Point out why an unbeliever cannot be sanctified.
12. Why will false teaching cause difficulties in my sanctification?
13. What has obedience to do with my sanctification?
14. State the reason why my daily renewal is impossible without forgiveness of sins.
15. Give a description of the sanctified life.
16. Who will be raised from the dead?
17. Who shall inherit eternal life?
18. What does the Bible tell about eternal life?
19. What will happen to those who are not God's children?
20. State the first two lessons in the study of God's way of salvation.

BIBLE STUDY

Read Matt. 5:1-12 and do the following work:

1. Make a list of the marks of those whom Jesus calls blessed;
2. Make a list of the blessings that they are to receive;
3. Give a description of (1) the poor in spirit; (2) those that mourn; (3) the meek; (4) those that hunger and thirst after righteousness; (5) the merciful; (6) the pure in heart; (7) the peacemakers; (8) those that are persecuted for righteousness' sake.
4. Point out the effect the life of such people would have in the home, the church, and the state.

CHAPTER TWENTY-SEVEN

The Lord's Prayer

Our Father, who art in heaven, hallowed be Thy name. Thy kingdom come. Thy will be done on earth, as it is in heaven. Give us this day our daily bread. And forgive us our trespasses, as we forgive those who trespass against us. And lead us not into temptation. But deliver us from evil. For Thine is the kingdom, and the power, and the glory, for ever and ever. Amen

The Third Main Part of the Catechism consists of the Lord's Prayer. This prayer is so named because the Lord Himself taught it to His disciples. It is divided into three parts—an introduction, seven petitions, and a conclusion.

1. PRAYER IS UNIVERSAL

Prayer is universal. Prayer is common to Christians and non-Christians alike.

Disappointment and sorrow and sickness and death are the common lot of all mankind. Neither health nor money nor power nor friends can cure sorrow nor stop death. In his helplessness man prays. He seeks the help of one who is stronger than himself.

2. CHRISTIAN PRAYER

Not all prayers are Christian prayers. In order to be Christian the prayer must be to the Christian God. And the Christian God is He whom Jesus Christ revealed as His Father.

Besides being a prayer to the Father of the Lord Jesus Christ, a Christian prayer is a prayer in Jesus' name.

3. PRAYER IN JESUS' NAME

When I pray in Jesus' name, I do not ask that my petitions be granted because I have deserved it, but because Christ has deserved it. He is my Savior and His privileges are my privileges. It is for His sake I ask God to hear my prayer.

Whatsoever ye shall ask in My name that will I do, that the Father may be glorified in the Son (John 14:13).

4. GOD ANSWERS PRAYER

I know that God will answer my prayers because He has promised to do so. Jesus said:

Ask, and it shall be given you; seek, and ye shall find; knock, and it shall be opened unto you (Matt. 7:7):

When I pray to my heavenly Father I do not tell Him anything that He does not know. I simply open my heart to Him and give Him the opportunity to help me.

Your Father knoweth what things ye have need of, before ye ask Him (Matt. 6:8).

Does God always answer my prayer? He does, but sometimes He says, No

I am so short-sighted and sinful that I may pray for things that would harm me. God said no to Paul when he asked that the thorn in the flesh be taken from him (II Cor. 12:7-9). When God says no, He always gives what is better, though it may take time before we see it.

We know not how to pray as we ought; but the Spirit Himself maketh intercession for us with groanings which cannot be uttered (Rom. 8:26).

5. HONESTY AND SIMPLICITY IN PRAYER

Prayer must be honest. We cannot fool God.

When ye pray, ye shall not be as the hypocrites (Matt. 6:5).

Honesty and simplicity go together. God does not hear us for the sake of the many words or because we repeat the same words again and again.

In praying, use not vain repetitions, as the Gentiles do: for they think that they shall be heard for their much speaking (Matt. 6:7).

117

6. PRAY ALWAYS

When we love God, there is an undercurrent in our heart that always is turned toward God and always seeks Him. How often a thought or a few silent words will ascend to God even during the busiest moments.

Pray without ceasing (I Thess. 5:17).

> Prayer is the soul's sincere desire,
> Unuttered or expressed;
> The motion of a hidden fire
> That trembles in the breast.
>
> Prayer is the burden of a sigh,
> The falling of a tear,
> The upward glancing of the eye
> When none but God is near.
>
> (L. H., No. 361. vv. 1 and 2)

At the same time God's people will have their regular times for prayer. Morning and evening devotion, however brief, and grace at meals are spiritual necessities.

THE INTRODUCTION

Our Father, who art in heaven.

What does this mean?

Answer: God thereby tenderly encourages us to believe that He is truly our Father, and that we are truly His children, so that we may boldly and confidently come to Him in prayer, even as beloved children come to their dear father.

What a loving God you and I have.

He *tenderly* encourages us to believe that He is *truly* our Father . . . so that we *boldly* and *confidently* may come to Him in prayer.

Prayer to such a Father is a privilege and a joy. Here I meet understanding, sympathy, love, and readiness to help —everything that I need.

A living, growing Christian will also want to pray in his own words. He will have experiences and personal problems about which he wants to speak to the Lord. And the Lord's Prayer is not to be used mechanically till it becomes mere words thoughtlessly repeated. Still, a child of God will again and again find in the Lord's Prayer a most satisfactory form for what his soul seeks to express.[1]

---

[1]A special meaning has been ascribed to different postures. Folded hands signify confidence; bent knees, humility; standing indicates respect; lifted eyes and hands that we are ready to receive; bowed head and downcast eyes, unworthiness.

7. FELLOWSHIP IN PRAYER

In the Lord's Prayer we say our Father, not my Father. No child of God stands alone. He belongs to the communion of saints, the great fellowship of God's people. All those who belong to this fellowship meet daily before the throne of God, each one praying for himself and for all the others. It is the brotherhood of praying hearts.

Christ gave a special promise to this praying brotherhood. *I say unto you, that if two of you shall agree on earth as touching anything that they shall ask, it shall be done for them of My Father who is in heaven* (Matt. 18:19).

Prayer:

Dear God, our Father in Christ Jesus, teach us to pray. Give us Thy Holy Spirit that we may learn to pray according to Thy will. Give us joy in praying to Thee. Fulfill Thy rich promises to us and to all Thy children. In Jesus' name. Amen.

QUESTIONS
(To be answered in writing, except 1 and 2)

1. Look up and read in your Bible the Bible passages quoted in this chapter. Underscore them in your Bible.
2. Be ready to recite the material that is to be memorized.
3. What does the Third Main Part of the Catechism deal with?
4. State the name of this prayer and why it has this name.
5. Explain why prayer is universal.
6. What makes a prayer a Christian prayer?
7. When do we pray in Jesus' name?
8. How do we know that God will answer our prayer?
9. Why does God sometimes say no to our prayer?
10. Who helps us to pray?
11. Explain (1) honesty in prayer, (2) simplicity in prayer.
12. How can we pray always?
13. Point out the importance of regular times for prayer.
14. Why is prayer to our heavenly Father a privilege and a joy?
15. How should the Lord's Prayer be prayed?
16. State the reason why a Christian at times wants to use his own words when praying.
17. Point out the benefits of fellowship in prayer.

BIBLE STUDY

Read Psalm 103:1-13 and point out (1) the leading thought of these verses; (2) the relation between verses 1 and 2 and verses 3 to 13; (3) what it means to bless God's name; (4) why David wants all that is in him to bless God; (5) the benefits enumerated in each of verses 3 to 13.

CHAPTER TWENTY-EIGHT

The First Three Petitions

As we now begin our study of the seven petitions, we will remember that each petition is a prayer. As we approach each petition, we, too, will pray: *Lord, teach us to pray* (Luke 11:1).

THE FIRST PETITION

Hallowed be Thy name.

What does this mean?

Answer: God's name is indeed holy in itself; but we pray in this petition that it may be hallowed also among us.

How is this done?

Answer: When the Word of God is taught in its truth and purity and we, as God's children, lead holy lives in accordance with it. This grant us, dear Father in heaven! But whoever teaches and lives otherwise than as God's Word teaches, profanes the name of God among us. From this preserve us, heavenly Father!

1. FIRST THINGS FIRST

The first three petitions deal with God, His name, His kingdom, and His will. This arrangement again shows the importance of placing first things first.

2. GOD'S NAME HOLY

God's name is holy because God is holy. Sin has placed its unclean marks on man, but it cannot reach God.

When Christ was here on earth, He was dealing with sinful men and surrounded by sin of all kinds, but not a dark spot was left on Him. We love Him the more for His holiness. God's people want to be like Him. When God calls them to be holy, they answer by praying: Create in me a clean heart, O God.

Ye shall be holy; for I the Lord your God am holy (Lev. 19:2).

3. HALLOWING GOD'S NAME

The Catechism says that God's name is hallowed among us when the Word of God is taught in its truth and purity, and we, as God's children, lead holy lives in accordance with it.

Only when we teach God's Word in its truth and purity, is the true and living God among us, and only then do we know the way of salvation.

Sanctify them in the truth; Thy word is truth (John 17: 17).

Living in accordance with God's Word is next in importance.

Be ye doers of the word, and not hearers only, deluding your own selves (James 1:22).

With our whole heart we join in the prayer: This grant us, dear Father in heaven!

4. PROFANING GOD'S NAME

False teaching and ungodly living profane God's name among us. If we teach otherwise than God's Word teaches, we abuse and corrupt God's Word as well as His way of salvation. And if we live as if sin were the highway to happiness, we are lying about God.

From this preserve us, heavenly Father!

THE SECOND PETITION

Thy kingdom come.

What does this mean?

Answer: The kingdom of God comes indeed of itself, without our prayer; but we pray in this petition that it may come also to us.

How is this done?

Answer: When our heavenly Father gives us His Holy Spirit, so that by His grace we believe His holy Word, and live a godly life here on earth and in heaven forever.

This is the mission prayer.

5. GOD'S KINGDOM

The kingdom of God is the kingdom Jesus founded and of which He is the king. Christ rules in the hearts of His people, over their thoughts, plans, and energy.

The kingdom of God is within you (Luke 17:21).

It does not consist in property, jobs, money, and pleasures. The kingdom of God offers real riches that last forever.

The kingdom of God is not eating and drinking, but righteousness and peace and joy in the Holy Spirit (Rom. 14:17).

6. THE KINGDOM IS GOD'S GIFT

The Catechism says that God's kingdom comes indeed without our prayer. So it does. God promised Adam and Eve a Savior; they did not ask for Him. Christ established the kingdom here on earth without our prayer. As the prophet said: "The zeal of the Lord of hosts will perform this" (Is. 9:7).

7. THE KINGDOM AND OUR PRAYERS

Christ becomes our king when we believe God's holy Word and live a godly life. This is the work of the Holy Spirit and we need to pray and to pray much that the Spirit will do this work in our hearts.

8. UNIVERSAL AND EVERLASTING KINGDOM

Christ came to be the Savior of all people and to establish His kingdom in every heart. So He said to His people: "Go ye, and make disciples of all nations." It is a task that calls for prayer and workers. "The harvest indeed is plenteous, but the laborers are few. Pray ye therefore the Lord of the harvest, that He send forth laborers into His harvest" (Matt. 9:37-38). And we know that

Of His kingdom there shall be no end (Luke 1:33).

THE THIRD PETITION

Thy will be done on earth, as it is heaven.

What does this mean?

Answer: The good and gracious will of God is done indeed without our prayer; but we pray in this petition that it may also be done among us.

How is this done?

Answer: When God destroys and brings to naught every evil counsel and purpose of the devil, the world, and our own flesh, which would hinder us from hallowing His name, and prevent the coming of His kingdom; and when He strengthens us and keeps us steadfast in His Word and in faith, even unto our end. This is His good and gracious will.

9. THE DIFFICULT PRAYER

Thy will be done, not mine. This causes no difficulty in heaven where the will of the angels and of the saints is the same as God's will. Not so on earth. Because of sin, our will is too often contrary to God's will.

In this petition we pray that our will may be in harmony with God's will. Only then are we going in the right direction. Only then do we experience the peace and power of God in our soul. Nothing else gives meaning to our life.

10. GOD'S WILL GOOD AND GRACIOUS

God's will is always good and gracious. He Himself has said:

I know the thoughts that I think toward you, saith the Lord, thoughts of peace, and not of evil (Jer. 29:11) .

It is God's will that sin shall not rule over us. Sin ruins man, his home, his church, and his country. God's will leads to victory over sin and to freedom. It builds Christian character and happiness

This is the will of God, even your sanctification (I Thess. 4:3) .

11. GOD'S HELP

It is the devil, the world, and our own flesh that lead us to rebel against God's will. They are strong forces, not to be overcome by our own will power and strength. We need to love God and His will if we shall conquer. Only the Holy Spirit can create this love and give the needed strength. He strengthens us by keeping us steadfast in God's Word and in faith in Jesus Christ. Constant fellowship with Christ in His Word gives the Holy Spirit the opportunity to help us.

Our conscience is in the center of the battle. It is the advance guard of our power to decide and to act. On the one hand are the desires and lusts of the devil, the world, and the flesh, working to make the conscience yield. On the other side are God's love and gracious will as we have learned to know them in His Word, urging the conscience

123

to be steadfast. The Holy Spirit will give us victory when we listen to the voice of God's Word and keep on praying: Thy will be done!

Prayer:

Our Father, who art in heaven, hallowed be Thy name. Thy kingdom come. Thy will be done on earth, as it is in heaven. Amen.

WORD STUDY

Profane: defile, misuse, "throw dirt upon." Delude: mislead, deceive.

QUESTIONS

(To be answered in writing, except 1 and 2)

1. Look up and read in your Bible the Bible passages quoted in this chapter. Underscore them in your Bible.
2. Be ready to recite the material that is to be memorized.
3. What do we mean when we say that Christ in the Lord's Prayer placed first things first?
4. How did Christ demonstrate God's holiness here on earth?
5. In what two ways do we hallow God's name?
6. How is God's name profaned?
7. In your opinion, what makes it a serious sin to profane God's name? (See Chap. Four, 2.)
8. Why do we call the Second Petition the mission prayer?
9. Explain the kingdom of God.
10. State the riches of the kingdom of God.
11. How can we say that God's kingdom comes without our prayer?
12. Why do we need to pray: Thy kingdom come?
13. How far did Christ want His kingdom to extend?
14. What is our share in this work?
15. Why is the Third Petition called the difficult prayer?
16. Point out the benefits to us when we are in harmony with God's will.
17. How can you prove that God's will is good and gracious?
18. What two forces struggle for mastery in our consciences?
19. How does God help us in this struggle?
20. From your own experience, describe this struggle in the conscience.

BIBLE STUDY

Read Psalm 87. (Rahab is Egypt. Selah means that the chorus pauses while the band continues to play. Such a pause comes at the end of an important truth. Zion was the hill in Jerusalem where the temple stood. Zion is a symbol of God's kingdom on earth, the holy Christian Church. The people mentioned are types, representatives of all nations.)

Point out (1) the vision the author has (begin with v. 6); (2) God's attitude to Zion; (3) the glorious things spoken of Zion; (4) the location of these nations; (5) the meaning of the words, born in Zion; (6) the meaning of the last half of v. 5; (7) why the nations rejoice.

124

CHAPTER TWENTY-NINE

The Fourth and Fifth Petitions

We have seen that the first three petitions deal with God's name, God's kingdom, and God's will. In the last four, our needs are placed before God.

THE FOURTH PETITION

Give us this day our daily bread.

What does this mean?

Answer: God indeed gives daily bread to all men, even to the wicked, without our prayer; but we pray in this petition that He would lead us to acknowledge our daily bread as His gift, and to receive it with thanksgiving.

What is meant by daily bread?

Answer: Everything that is required to satisfy our bodily needs; such as food and raiment, house and home, fields and flocks, money and goods; pious parents, children and servants; godly and faithful rulers, good government; seasonable weather, peace and health; order and honor; true friends, good neighbors, and the like.

1. THE PRAYER FOR DAILY BREAD

Daily bread, how important it is! The anxiety caused by sickness, crop failure, or unemployment is very real. It is natural to worry when the pocketbook is empty. So God invites us to take the problem of our daily bread to Him.

Casting all your anxiety upon Him, because He careth for you (I Peter 5:7).

Christ placed the petition for our daily bread in the center of the Lord's Prayer. It is the first of the petitions dealing with our needs. By placing it where He did, Christ recognized the importance of our daily bread even for our spiritual welfare. We must relieve our mind of all worry for the needs of our body in order to give attention to the needs of our soul.

It is also important that we realize the close connection between the first three petitions and the fourth. It is when God's name is hallowed, when His kingdom comes, and when His will is done, that the best opportunities exist for earning our daily bread.

2. WHAT IS DAILY BREAD?

Daily bread is everything that is required to satisfy our bodily needs. The Catechism list includes all that is necessary or profitable.

This prayer speaks not only of our own needs, but of the needs of our neighbor and of the whole nation as well. God wants us to remember that the individual does not fare well unless his neighbor and his nation also fare well.

3. GOD, THE GIVER OF DAILY BREAD

"God indeed gives daily bread to all men, even to the wicked, without our prayer." Every spring God sets His table for man and beast and covers it with an unending variety of food. It is my heavenly Father's table, and there He also feeds me and provides abundantly for all my needs.

This table is so large and so well provided and our heavenly Father is so good and gracious, that even the wicked are welcome to satisfy their hunger.

He maketh His sun to rise on the evil and the good, and sendeth rain on the just and the unjust (Matt. 5:45).

4. THIS DAY

God provides for each day as it comes. He will take care of tomorrow as He takes care of today. If we live as His children we can safely leave the future in His hands.

Be not therefore anxious for the morrow (Matt. 6:34).

5. DAILY BREAD BECOMES OURS THROUGH WORK

There is neither food nor clothing in laziness. Work teaches the value of what God gives. Only the worker appreciates the opportunity to earn a living. (See Chap. Nine, 4.)

6. THANKSGIVING FOR DAILY BREAD

"We pray in this petition that He would lead us to acknowledge our daily bread as His gift, and to receive it with thanksgiving."

Lack of appreciation and gratitude is a mark of a generation that has turned away from God. "Knowing God, they glorified Him not as God, neither gave thanks" (Rom. 1:21). Thankless people are not happy people. Gratitude makes people both happy and content.

THE FIFTH PETITION

And forgive us our trespasses, as we forgive those who trespass against us.

What does this mean?

Answer: We pray in this petition, that our heavenly Father would not regard our sins nor because of them deny our prayers; for we neither merit, nor deserve those things for which we pray; but that He would grant us all things through grace, even though we sin daily, and deserve nothing but punishment. And certainly we, on our part, will heartily forgive, and gladly do good to those who may sin against us.

(Before proceeding review Chap. Twenty-three.)

7. OUR FOREMOST SPIRITUAL NEED

Having presented the petition for our daily bread, the Lord's Prayer turns to our spiritual needs. First and foremost among these is the forgiveness of our sins.

In our life, sin is an ever disturbing element. We recognize its ugly form in the wrong we do as well as in the good we neglect to do. It forces itself into our relation to God, and our relation to man is distorted by it. It chills and deadens our faith, love, and obedience, and it breeds evil desires.

8. DIFFERENT TERMS FOR SIN

The Bible uses several terms for sin. The most general name is sin, but it is also called trespass, transgression, iniquity, and debt. In the Fifth Petition it is called trespass, in order to emphasize that we not only are owing God a debt that we cannot pay, but that we have incurred guilt and condemnation. We have broken God's law.

9. WE DESERVE NOTHING BUT PUNISHMENT

"We sin daily, and deserve nothing but punishment." Luther speaks of the same kind of sin that the apostle has in mind when he says:

The good which I would I do not; but the evil which I would not, that I practice (Rom. 7:19).

The apostle does not speak of wilful sin, but of the evil thoughts that come and go, of evil desires that still appear in the heart; of pride, jealousy, and unbelief; of lukewarm love and joyless obedience; and of lifeless interest and half hearted prayers. And to a Christian all such things are sin.

10. THE WORD "AND"

When we pray for our daily bread, the question at once arises, How can God give all these blessings to us who deserve nothing but punishment?

Christ recognizes our difficulty and in order to remove our fear, He ties the petition for the forgiveness of our sins to the petition for daily bread by the little word "and." It is as if He would say, Do not fear to ask God for your daily bread; just ask Him to forgive your sins, and He will do it and give you all the other things also.

11. WE WILL ALSO FORGIVE

"And certainly we, on our part, will heartily forgive, and gladly do good to those who may sin against us."

For if ye forgive men their trespasses, your heavenly Father will also forgive you. But if ye forgive not men their trespasses, neither will your Father forgive your trespasses (Matt. 6:14-15).

We do not forgive others as a payment for God's forgiveness of our sins, neither do we first forgive others in order that God then may forgive us. We forgive others in gratitude to God for His forgiveness.

On the other hand, if we do not forgive others it shows that we are not willing to give up the sin of hatred and revenge. As a result, our heart is closed to God's forgiveness.

Prayer:

Father, we thank Thee that Thou hast invited us to bring all our bodily needs to Thee. We also thank Thee that Thou hast promised to take care of us. Help us to trust Thee.

We who sin daily against Thee need much forgiveness. We thank Thee that Thou art always willing to forgive when we confess our sins to Thee. Help us to be just as willing to forgive those who sin against us. In Jesus' name. Amen.

QUESTIONS

(To be answered in writing, except 1 and 2)

1. Look up and read in your Bible all the Bible passages quoted in this chapter. Underscore them in your Bible.
2. Be ready to recite the material that is to be memorized.
3. Why does God invite us to speak to Him about our daily bread?
4. Point out the connection between the first three petitions and the fourth one.
5. Why did Christ place the petition for daily bread in the center of the Lord's Prayer?
6. Give the reason why we should pray for daily bread for others as well as for ourselves.
7. How does God provide our daily bread?
8. Why did Christ add the words "this day"?
9. How does the bread God provides become our bread?
10. What has thanksgiving to do with our daily bread?
11. Why is the forgiveness of sins our foremost spiritual need?
12. State the different words the Bible uses for sin.
13. Why is the word trespass used in the Fifth Petition?
14. Point out sins found even in God's children.
15. State the reason why the Fifth Petition begins with the word "And."
16. Why can we not retain God's forgiveness if we do not forgive others?

BIBLE STUDY

Read Matt. 18:23-35 and explain (1) why Jesus told this parable, (2) who is the one who owed ten thousand talents and to whom did he owe it, (3) who owed the hundred shillings and to whom, (4) why he who had a hundred shillings coming, would not forgive his debtor when he had received so much forgiveness himself, and (5) how this parable illustrates the Fifth Petition. (Ten thousand talents would probably be about ten million dollars in our money, and a hundred shillings about seventeen dollars.)

CHAPTER THIRTY

The Sixth and Seventh Petitions and the Conclusion

THE SIXTH PETITION

And lead us not into temptation

What does this mean?

Answer: God indeed tempts no one to sin; but we pray in this petition that God would so guard and preserve us, that the .devil, the world, and our own flesh may not deceive us, nor lead us into error and unbelief, despair, and other great and shameful sins; but that, when so tempted, we may finally prevail and gain victory.

(Before proceeding Chap. Twenty-six should be reviewed.)

1. FUTURE PERILS

Again we meet the little word "and," closely tying this petition to the fifth and the fourth. It is the same fear on our part that Christ meets in this petition as in the fifth. There the fear was caused by past and present sins, here it is the thought of future sins that brings anxiety.

Yes, I believe that God forgives the sins I have done and that He, because of them, will not deny my prayers. But what about tomorrow and the next day and the next? I know something about my own weaknesses, and the cunning and power of my enemies. I am afraid that I will be overpowered by sin, that my prayers will not be heard, and that everything will be lost.

130

So Christ teaches us also to place our future difficulties in our heavenly Father's hand.

2. TEMPTATIONS ARE OPPORTUNITIES

."God indeed tempts no one to sin."

My life is in my Father's hand. "He leadeth me." The road is at times rough and slippery. Sin has made it so. However, it is necessary for my spiritual development and growth that I learn to negotiate the treacherous stretches. My faith, my love, my watchfulness, my prayers, are all brought into play. A miscalculation may mean serious trouble.

There are many such stretches on the road of life. I may make a detour around some of them, but not around all.

The danger comes from the devil, the world, and my own flesh, not from God. He does not tempt us to sin. The rough spots are opportunities He presents to us. This is the reason why James says: "Count it all joy, my brethren, when ye fall into manifold temptations; knowing that the proving of your faith worketh patience" (James 1:2-3).

The word "fall" means to enter into, not to fall in sin.

3. BE WATCHFUL

It is the enemies that make the traveling dangerous. They may deceive us into thinking that the road is not slippery. Or they may lead us into error and unbelief so that we do not pay attention to the guideposts of the Word of God. Or they may lead us to take chances, trusting our luck. This is their preliminary work. Then when things go wrong, despair comes like a highway robber, killing the hope of God's grace that may be left in our soul, and leading us into more shameful sins.

My son, if sinners entice thee, consent thou not (Prov. 1:10).

Watch and pray, that ye enter not into temptation (Matt. 26:41).

4. GOD IS OUR HELPER

"We pray in this petition that God would so guard and preserve us, that ... when so tempted, we may finally prevail and gain victory."

It is God that must guard and preserve us from sin. We cannot do it ourselves. Through the means of grace the

Holy Spirit sanctifies the whole Christian Church on earth, and preserves it in union with Jesus Christ in the one true faith, as we learned in the Third Article. And this is what we, in the Sixth Petition, ask Him to do for us

THE SEVENTH PETITION

But deliver us from evil.

What does this mean?

Answer: We pray in this petition, as in a summary, that our heavenly Father would deliver us from all manner of evil, whether it affects the body or soul, property or reputation, and at last, when the hour of death shall come, grant us a blessed end, and graciously take us from this world of sorrow to Himself in heaven.

5. BUT DELIVER US

The Seventh Petition begins with the word "but," closely connecting it with the Sixth. The thought is, And lead us not into temptation, but on the contrary, deliver us from evil.

Every petition has been a prayer for some specific gift of grace; now the last one concludes by asking, as in a summary, deliverance from all evil. This petition teaches us that it is not necessary always to specify our needs in detail. Our Father knows what we need, even better than we do.

6. EVILS CAUSED BY SIN

The Fifth and the Sixth Petitions deal with the chief evil, sin. This petition deals with the evil consequences of sin. They are evident everywhere in our life.

Sickness, accidents, pain, broken health, poverty are some of the evils which affect our body.

A destroyed will power, a perverted, blinded mind, an evil conscience affect our soul.

Theft, fraud, fire, floods, wars, and the like may ruin our property.

Slander, lies, false accusations, and disgrace may destroy our reputation.

Truly, the world is full of evil. We need to pray: Deliver us from evil.

7. GOD'S PROMISES

God answers this, as every other prayer, in His own way. He knows what is best for our spiritual welfare. Every one that trusts Him will experience that our heavenly Father is faithful and keeps His promises.

"Yea, though I walk through the valley of the shadow of death, I will fear no evil; for Thou art with me" (Ps. 23:4). The walk through the valley of the shadow of death is a part of the experience of God's children as of everybody else. But we can trust His promises.

The Lord will keep thee from all evil (Ps. 121:7).

The Lord will deliver me from every evil work, and will save me unto His heavenly kingdom (II Tim. 4:18).

THE CONCLUSION

For Thine is the kingdom, and the power, and the glory, for ever and ever. Amen

What does the word "Amen" mean?

Answer: It means that I should be assured that such petitions are acceptable to our heavenly Father, and are heard by Him; for He Himself has commanded us to pray in this manner, and has promised to hear us. Amen, Amen, that is, Yea, yea, it shall be so.

In these concluding words, Christ gives three reasons why we should pray with all cheerfulness and confidence.

For Thine is the kingdom—the kingdom for which we pray and to which we belong, is God's kingdom. Surely He will take care of it.

And the power—God has the power needed to answer our prayers.

And the glory—when He answers, the glory is His, not ours.

And so it is and will be for ever and ever.

Hallelujah, salvation, and glory, and power, belong to our God (Rev. 19:1).

The word *Amen* means verily, truly. Christ used it as a strong word of assurance (John 3:3, 5; 16:23). It is an added encouragement to pray and an added assurance that our Father in heaven will hear us.

☆   ☆

And so we have completed the third lesson in our study of God's way of salvation. The Ten Commandments taught us the first lesson. We are lost and condemned sinners every one. The Creed supplied the second lesson. In His unspeakable love, God our Father sent His Son to die for our sins;

and the Holy Spirit, through Word and Sacraments, is working faith in Jesus Christ. The third lesson teaches us that prayer is necessary if we are to live and die as God's children. The Holy Spirit cannot do His work in a heart that refuses to draw nigh unto God in prayer.

Prayer:
Praise to the Lord! O let all that is in me adore Him!
All that hath life and breath, come now with praises before Him!
Let the Amen
Sound from His people again;
Gladly for aye we adore Him. Amen.

(L. H., No. 5, v. 5)

QUESTIONS
(To be answered in writing, except 1 and 2)

1. Look up and read in your Bible the Bible passages quoted in this chapter. Underscore them in your Bible
2. Be ready to recite the material that is to be memorized.
3. Why does the Sixth Petition begin with "And"?
4. How can we say that temptations are opportunities?
5. Who tempts us to sin?
6. Why is it necessary to watch and pray?
7. How does the Holy Spirit guard and preserve us from sin?
8. Why does the Seventh Petition begin with "But"?
9. Point out the four groups of evil mentioned in Luther's explanation to the Seventh Petition.
10. Make a list of evils from which God has delivered you.
11. Explain why Christ added the words: For Thine is the kingdom, etc.
12. Why is "Amen" added?
13. Read first Luther's explanation to the Introduction and then his explanation to the Conclusion, and state (1) what we should believe according to the first; (2) of what we should be assured according to the last; (3) how this applies to all our prayers.
14. How have these studies of the Lord's Prayer helped your own prayer life?
15. What three lessons have we learned in our study of God's way of salvation?

BIBLE STUDY

Read Matt. 26:31-35 and 69-75, and point out (1) why Jesus warned Peter; (2) what made Peter sure of the outcome; (3) to what extent he knew himself; (4) what moved Peter to enter the high priest's courtyard; (5) the accusations made by the servants; (6) the fear that took hold of Peter (see also John 18:26); (7) how many times he denied his Lord; (8) how strongly he denied Him; (9) what brought Peter to his senses (see also Luke 22:61); (10) why he went out and wept bitterly.

134

CHAPTER THIRTY-ONE

The Sacrament of Baptism

The Word and the Sacraments are the means the
Holy Spirit uses in His work to save man. We
have been studying the Word and the use the
Holy Spirit makes of it. We come now to the Sacraments, Baptism and the Lord's Supper.

Before proceeding with our study of Baptism,
the word Sacrament requires our attention.

1. THINGS IN COMMON

The Sacraments have three things in common. Both are
instituted by Christ; both use visible, material means, water
in Baptism, and bread and wine in the Lord's Supper; and
both give and bestow God's saving grace.

Other religious ordinances, such as confirmation, marriage, and ordination, have not all of these three features,
and, therefore, we do not accept them as Sacraments.[1]

*A definition: A sacrament is a holy act, instituted by
Christ Himself, in which He gives and bestows His saving
grace through the use of visible, material means.*

The Sacraments have also another thing in common.
Both require faith on the part of the one to whom the Sacrament is administered.

2. DIFFERENCE BETWEEN THE WORD AND THE SACRAMENTS

The difference between the Word and the Sacraments is
not that each brings to us a different part of God's saving

[1] The Roman Catholic Church teaches seven sacraments: Baptism, Confirmation, Confession, the Lord's Supper, Ordination, Marriage, and Extreme Unction.

grace, but that each is a different means for the giving of the same grace. God's saving grace cannot be split up into parts. When God's saving grace comes to man, it is always the full grace, even though we may make only partial use of it.

3. THE NEED THE SACRAMENTS MEET

Christ instituted the Sacraments in order to meet a need in those who were to be saved. What is this need?

As God's children, we want to be pure in heart and to love our Lord and our neighbor. Alas, too often we find neither purity nor love in our hearts. We find pride and jealousy and love of sinning. And the longer we live in fellowship with a Savior who loves holiness, the clearer do we see our own sinfulness. As the days go by we need more forgiveness, not less.

Having received God's forgiveness over and over again, we at times find it difficult to believe that God loves and forgives us even today. Now, it is this fact that He loves and forgives us even today that God wants us firmly to believe. Our peace, joy, strength, and victory depend upon a firm faith in God's love and forgiveness.

So Christ gave the Sacraments, where He deals with each one in a special and personal manner.

4. HOW THE SACRAMENTS MEET OUR NEED

In Baptism, God, so to speak, gave me a blank check on all His love, grace, and goodness. As His child I can draw on Him for all my needs. He bound Himself never to turn me down or to withdraw His promises. I was given free admission and full use of His boundless stores of forgiveness, support, and care. When I fail, and sin and doubt beset me, God invites me to take refuge in His covenant and make use of the privileges that He has granted me. God's covenant stands today and every day in spite of my sins.

And whenever I partake of the Lord's Supper, He gives me His body and blood with the forgiveness of my sins and thus assures me personally that He still loves and forgives me.

Thus Christ, through the Sacraments, helps my weak and struggling faith in Him to grow and become strong enough for the task of the day.

5. MISUSING THE SACRAMENTS

The Sacraments may be misused. I may comfort myself with the fact that I am baptized and that I partake of the Lord's Supper though I do not love and serve my Lord and Savior and do not want to repent of my sins. Then I misuse the Sacraments. Christ gave the Sacraments as means for holy living. They were not given to furnish false security for unrepenting sinners.

BAPTISM

As in the case of everything else in the New Testament, Baptism also had its preparation in the Old Testament.

6. OLD TESTAMENT TYPE

Baptism has taken the place of circumcision as an act establishing a covenant between God and the individual. When the eight-day-old child was circumcised, God took him into the covenant He had established with Abraham and his descendants. Jehovah, the covenant God, now became the child's God. All Jehovah's promises belonged from then on to the child and would be fulfilled upon him. As a result, all the obligations and duties of the covenant also rested upon the child. All this, and more, is now accomplished in Baptism.

"Ye were also circumcised with a circumcision not made with hands . . . in the circumcision of Christ; having been buried with Him in Baptism, wherein ye were also raised with Him through faith in the working of God, who raised Him from the dead" (Col. 2:11-12).

7. OLD TESTAMENT CLEANSINGS

There was also another development preparing for the New Testament Baptism. It was connected with the teaching of two fundamental truths, sin and forgiveness.

In order to teach Israel that sin had penetrated the whole man and made him unclean in God's sight, God not only gave them minute rules for their daily life, but He also provided means for their cleansing. Without such cleansing they could not appear before Him. Washing was a prominent part of the cleansing ritual (Gen. 35:2; Ex. 19:10; Lev. 15). The act was symbolic, signifying cleansing from spiritual uncleanness by the means God had provided.

When it is said that God would wash away the filth of the people, the meaning is that He would forgive their sins. (See Is. 4:4; Ezek. 36:25.)

8. DEVELOPMENTS

It was a natural result of these Old Testament teachings and practices that the Jews baptized the Gentiles who were converted to the Jewish faith. It was a symbolic act signifying the washing away of all the impurities of the heathen life.

John's baptism was the last step in the Old Testament preparation for the New Testament Baptism. At God's command, he baptized the Jews who confessed their sins. His baptism was a testimony from God that the Jews, and not the Gentiles alone, needed repentance and forgiveness of sins.

The Baptism Jesus instituted completed the development. It gives what the previous washings and baptisms pointed forward to. The difference between John's baptism and Jesus' Baptism is stated by John himself.

I indeed baptize you in water unto repentance; but He that cometh after me is mightier than I, whose shoes I am not worthy to bear; He shall baptize you in the Holy Spirit and in fire (Matt. 3:11).

In the Baptism instituted by Christ the Holy Spirit would be at work to save and to sanctify.

Prayer:

I thank Thee, my God and Father, for my Baptism and for the covenant Thou didst establish with me. Though I have failed more than words can say, Thou hast not failed and never will fail. Thou hast kept Thy promises. Thy love and forgiveness are the same even today, and for this I thank Thee. Grant me to trust Thee more fully and serve Thee more honestly. In Jesus' name. Amen.

QUESTIONS
(To be answered in writing, except 1 and 2)

1. Look up and read in your Bible the Bible passages quoted in this chapter. Underscore them in your Bible
2. Be ready to recite the material that is to be memorized.
3. What means does the Holy Spirit use in His work to save man?
4. How many Sacraments do we have in the Lutheran Church? Name them.

5. State the three things that the Sacraments have in common.
6. What do the Sacraments require on the part of man?
7. Point out the difference between the Word and the Sacraments as means of grace.
8. Why do we need Sacraments?
9. How do the Sacraments meet our spiritual need?
10. In what way may the Sacraments be misused?
11. How was circumcision a type of Baptism?
12. State the purpose of the Old Testament cleansings.
13. Why were gentiles baptized when they accepted the Jewish faith?
14. What new feature did John's baptism introduce?
15. Point out the difference between John's baptism and the Baptism instituted by Christ.

BIBLE STUDY

Read Luke 3:1-17 and answer the following questions: (1) Who sent John to preach baptism of repentance? (2) What is "baptism of repentance"? (3) According to Isaiah, quoted in Luke 3:4-6, what was the purpose of John's work? (4) Comparing verses 8 and 10-14, what are "fruits worthy of repentance"? (5) What difference did John say that there was between himself and Christ and between his work and the work of Christ?

CHAPTER THIRTY-TWO

New Testament Baptism

We have had a glimpse of the Old Testament background for Baptism. What does the New Testament teach regarding Baptism? Let us take the questions and answers in the Catechism and see how they harmonize with the New Testament. May the Holy Spirit help us more fully to realize the value of our Baptism.

1. BAPTISM IN THE NAME OF THE TRIUNE GOD

What is Baptism?

Answer: Baptism is not simply water, but it is the water used according to God's command and connected with God's word

What is this word of God?

Answer: It is the word of our Lord Jesus Christ, as recorded in the last chapter of Matthew:

Go ye therefore, and make disciples of all the nations, baptizing them into the name of the Father, and of the Son, and of the Holy Spirit.

It is Jesus Christ who has commanded to baptize into the name of the Father, and of the Son, and of the Holy Spirit.

To baptize into the name of the Triune God means that in Baptism we are brought into fellowship with God. We are made members of God's family. He becomes our God and we become His children.

2. BENEFITS OF BAPTISM

What gifts or benefits does Baptism bestow?

Answer: It works forgiveness of sins, delivers from death and the devil, and gives everlasting salvation to all who believe, as the word and the promise of God declares.

What is this word and promise of God?

Answer: It is the word of our Lord Jesus Christ, as recorded in the last chapter of Mark:

He that believeth and is baptized shall be saved; but he that believeth not shall be damned.

3. FORGIVENESS AND SALVATION THROUGH BAPTISM

The Catechism says that Baptism works forgiveness. This is the Bible's teaching. When the Jews on Pentecost Sunday asked what they should do, Peter answered:

Repent ye, and be baptized every one of you in the name of Jesus Christ unto the remission of your sins; and ye shall receive the gift of the Holy Spirit (Acts 2:38).

Ananias said to Paul:

Arise, and be baptized, and wash away thy sins (Acts 22:16).

To the Galatians the apostle Paul writes:

As many of you as were baptized into Christ did put on Christ (Gal. 3:27).

In Baptism they put on Christ. To put on Christ means that He covers us with His righteousness as with a dress. Our sins are taken away. Christ, with everything He has, is ours. The Bible expresses it by saying that we are in Christ. We stand before God, not as we are in ourselves, but as we are in Him. His full salvation is ours.

Peter summarizes this Bible truth when he says that Baptism saves. He reminds his readers that the water of the flood carried the ark to safety with those that were in it. The water of the flood was a type of the water of Baptism.

Which also after a true likeness doth now save you, even Baptism (I Peter 3:21)

So God, through Baptism, forgives sins and gives everlasting salvation to all who believe Christ's word.

4. WATER AND WORD

How can water do such great things?

Answer: It is not water, indeed, that does such great things, but the word of God connected with the water, and our faith which re-

lies on that word of God. For without the word of God, it is simply water and no Baptism. But when connected with the word of God, it is a Baptism, that is, a gracious water of life and a washing of regeneration in the Holy Ghost, as St. Paul says to Titus, in the third chapter.

According to His mercy He saved us, by the washing of regeneration, and renewing of the Holy Ghost; which He shed on us abundantly through Jesus Christ our Savior; that being justified by His grace, we should be made heirs according to the hope of eternal life. This is a faithful saying (Tit. 3:4-8).

CHRIST'S WORD MAKES BAPTISM

We could not baptize a person without the use of water. Still, the use of water would not be Baptism without the word Christ spoke when He instituted Baptism. For the power to save is in the word of Christ, who has all authority in heaven and on earth. Because of these words of Christ, God's saving grace is present and offered in every Baptism.

Whether or not Baptism becomes a washing of regeneration and renewing of the Holy Spirit to him who is baptized, depends upon whether or not he believes the word of Christ. According to God's Word no one is saved who does not believe in Christ.

5. WHAT BAPTISM SIGNIFIES

What does such Baptism with water signify?

Answer: It signifies that the old Adam in us, together with all sins and evil lusts, should be drowned by daily sorrow and repentance, and be put to death; and that the new man should daily come forth and rise, to live before God in righteousness and holiness forever.

Where is it so written?

Answer: St. Paul, in the sixth chapter of the Epistle to the Romans, says:

We are buried with Christ by Baptism into death, that like as He was raised up from the dead by the glory of the Father, even so we also should walk in newness of life.

142

6. THE OLD MUST DIE, THE NEW LIVE

In every true Christian there is something old and something new. The old is evil desire and love of sinning. The new is love to God and hatred of sin. The Bible calls these two natures the old man or old Adam, and the new man.

My old Adam is put to death when I am grieved over my evil thoughts and deeds and ask God to forgive me and cleanse me. By thus fighting down the evil temptations the old is being put to death and the new comes forth and lives. This is a real fight, for the evil lusts do not give in without a struggle. It is to this fight that all baptized people are called.

Fight the good fight of faith (I Tim. 6:12).

This is a daily fight. Not a day passes but that some evil desire tries to make me do what is sin. It is necessary that I make up my mind to fight the good fight of faith. Without the decision to live as a child of God no one will do it. And the decision must be renewed from day to day.

This is the program God gave me in my Baptism.

7. A THREEFOLD BLESSING

A threefold blessing came to me through my Baptism.

A. My sins were forgiven and I was made a member of God's family. I was born anew

B. God established His covenant with me personally. The mountains may depart, but my heavenly Father's covenant shall not be removed.

C. He gave me a program for my life.

8. THE MODE OF BAPTISM

What mode of Baptism should be used, immersion, or pouring, or sprinkling?

Sprinkling is an unsatisfactory term. We do not sprinkle the water on the one that is being baptized; we pour it by taking the water in the hollow of the hand.

Both immersion and pouring have been used during the entire history of the church. The question is not how much water is used, but that it is used according to God's command and connected with God's word. We pour the water over the crown of the head, this being the seat of man's intellectual powers. Pouring is used for practical reasons.[1]

Prayer:

Baptized into Thy name,
We all have Christ put on:
O may Thy love our hearts inflame
The course of truth to run.

May earthly feelings die,
And fruits of faith increase;
And Adam's nature prostrate lie
Before the Prince of Peace.

Endue us, Lord, with strength,
To triumph over sin:
That we may with Thy saints at length
Eternal glory win. Amen.

(L. H. No. 69, vv. 2-4)

QUESTIONS

(To be answered in writing, except 1 and 2)

1. Look up and read in your Bible the Bible passages quoted in this chapter. Underscore them in your Bible.
2. Be ready to recite the material that is to be memorized.
3. Who instituted Baptism?
4. Give the words of institution as recorded in Matt. 28:18-20.
5. What does it mean to baptize into the name of the Father and of the Son and of the Holy Spirit?
6. What are the benefits of Baptism?
7. Give Scripture proofs that Baptism works forgiveness of sin.
8. Explain the meaning of "did put on Christ."
9. How can it be said that Baptism saves?
10. Explain the words "washing of regeneration."
11. What makes Baptism a washing of regeneration?
12. Explain the term "the old Adam."
13. Why should a baptized person put old Adam to death?
14. How is the old Adam put to death?
15. What is meant by "the new man"?
16. How is the new man made to come forth and live before God?
17. What is the good fight of faith?

---

[1]There are many historical evidences proving that the early Church also used pouring. We shall mention three: (1) "The Twelve Apostles' Teaching," a little book written about the year 120 A. D., says that if there is not enough water for immersion then "pour water three times over the head in the name of the Father, the Son, and the Holy Spirit"; (2) a baptismal font from about the year 200 A. D. in the cathedral church at Syracus, Sicily, holds only about two gallons. Baptism here was of course by pouring; (3) the illustrations in the catacombs in Rome from the times when the Christians were persecuted, show Baptism performed by pouring. Even Jesus is shown standing in the river, the water being poured over Him. Though this may be claimed to be merely the idea of the artist, it nevertheless shows that pouring was an accepted practice.

144

18. Why is this a daily fight?
19. State the threefold blessing that came to you in Baptism.
20. Which mode of Baptism should be used? Give reasons.

BIBLE STUDY

After reading Rom. 6:1-4, state (1) the meaning of the words "continue in sin"; (2) why a Christian should not continue in sin; (3) the meaning of the words "died to sin"; (4) when they died to sin; (5) the relation to Christ established in Baptism; (6) the life a baptized person should live.

CHAPTER THIRTY-THREE

Infant Baptism

In the kingdom of heaven are many mysteries that the human mind cannot understand. Infant Baptism is one of them. The question for a Christian is not, Can I explain the mystery? The question is, Does God's Word teach it? A Christian wants above all to be obedient to God's Word.

1. THREE REASONS

We baptize infants for three Biblical reasons.

In the first place, a newborn baby has the same sinful nature that a grown person has. It is a sinner that needs salvation.

In the second place, baby needs to be born anew in order to become a member of the kingdom of heaven.

In the third place, the Holy Spirit through Baptism washes away sins, creates a new life, and saves.

2. BABY IS A SINNER

There is a universal law of heredity at work in the human family.

That which is born of the flesh is flesh; and that which is born of the Spirit is spirit (John 3:6).

By flesh Jesus means sinful human nature. We are all born with sinful natures, because we are all born of parents having sinful natures. Sinfulness is universal.

All have sinned and fall short of the glory of God (Rom. 3:23).

146

We were by nature children of wrath even as the rest
(Eph. 2:3).

To be children of wrath means to be under the condemnation of sin. There is no exception.

Our experience harmonizes with God's Word. We need not teach baby to be selfish, become angry, and "to start a rumpus" in order to get what it wants. Such things come of themselves without any training or coaxing.

And another thing. Jesus teaches that evil thoughts, murders, adulteries, theft and other vices come out of the heart. If the child's heart at birth has not these evil tendencies, at what time does such a radical change take place?

3. BABY NEEDS TO BE BORN ANEW

To Nicodemus Jesus said:

Verily, verily, I say unto thee, Except one be born anew, he cannot see the kingdom of God (John 3:3).

Jesus makes no exception. Everyone needs a new birth in order to enter God's kingdom. It is a universal law. And we notice how emphatic Jesus makes it.

4. BABY MUST BE BAPTIZED

God's Word teaches that through Baptism sins are washed away, new life is created, and the sinner saved. (See Chap. Thirty-two, 2 and 3.)

Christian parents want baby to share in this salvation. So, in obedience to Christ's command and trusting His word, baby is baptized into the name of the Father and of the Son and of the Holy Spirit.

5. BABY'S FAITH

What about baby's faith? The newborn child cannot be instructed. It cannot understand. Can it then believe?

Jesus said that babies can believe. Some mothers brought their little ones to Jesus that He should touch them. Luke calls them babes (Luke 18:15). The disciples thought that the kingdom of God was only for the grown-ups who could understand and reason and so believe. So they rebuked the mothers. But Jesus became indignant and said:

Verily, I say unto you, Whosoever shall not receive the kingdom of God as a little child, he shall in no wise enter therein (Luke 18:17).

Jesus said that a little child receives the kingdom of God. It is by faith and in no other way that we receive the kingdom of God. On another occasion Jesus warned against causing "one of these little ones that believe on Me to stumble" (Matt. 18:6).

It is not the children that must become knowing and understanding like the grown-ups in order to enter the kingdom. It is the grown-ups that must become like little children if they are to come in.

Verily I say unto you, Except ye turn, and become as little children, ye shall in no wise enter into the kingdom of heaven (Matt. 18:3).

Not only can little children believe in Christ, but it seems even less difficult for the Holy Spirit to create faith in the heart of a little child than in the heart of a grown person. As far as we can see, the reason is that the child offers no conscious resistance.

It is evident that the faith of a little child as yet is undeveloped. But so is everything else. It has intelligence, memory, ability to handle ideas, and all the other powers of the soul, though at first these powers are manifested only partly or not at all.[1]

6. UNBAPTIZED CHILDREN

The question is often asked, What happens to children who die without Baptism?

The Bible furnishes no direct answer to this question. We know that God is righteous and merciful as well as almighty and wise. We do not know what means He may have reserved for creating saving faith in children whom

---

[1] Infant Baptism is as old as the church. There are numerous evidences proving this fact. We shall mention four: (1) the church father Origen, who was born 185 A. D., says that the church has received the tradition from the apostles that children should be baptized; (2) Augustine, who was born 353 A. D., states that he had never read or heard that anyone who accepted the Old and New Testaments rejected infant Baptism; it rests on apostolic authority, he declares; (3) Pelagius, a contemporary of Augustine, makes the statement that he had never heard that even the false teachers denied that the Sacrament of Baptism should be given to children; (4) during the persecutions the early Roman Christians buried their dead in the catacombs. The inscriptions on the graves again and again state that children had been baptized. "Achilla, recently baptized, is buried here. He died one year and five months old." "Rufillo, recently baptized, lived three years and thirty days." "Aristus lived eight months. He was recently baptized." "Flavia Jovina lived three years and thirty-two days. She was recently baptized." Many others of a similar nature are found. (The persecutions lasted from about the middle of the first century to the year 311 A. D.)

He did not reach through Baptism. But we trust His wisdom and righteousness, and confidently believe that no one will be lost whom He could have saved

7. BAPTIZED CHILDREN WHO FALL AWAY

Those who are baptized as children but later fall away from God, should not be re-baptized when they again are converted. God has not broken His covenant, though man has.

When a baptized person who has fallen away from God later becomes converted, he is regenerated by the Word of God. For, as we have seen, each of God's means of grace brings to man the whole of God's saving grace.

Having been begotten again, not of corruptible seed, but of incorruptible, through the Word of God, which liveth and abideth (I Peter 1:23).

8. NOURISHMENT

The spiritual life of the children is nourished by instruction in the Word of God and by the Christian example of parents and others who exercise influence upon them.

It should be the normal course that baptized children grow up as God's children. But this growth cannot take place without nourishment

The instruction is of a special kind. It is an instruction in what Jesus commanded. But it is more than knowledge. The children must be taught to observe, that is, to do, to practice, all that Jesus commanded. Unless this is the result, the instruction does not become spiritual nourishment.

The parents are the children's first teachers. From the child's birth they impress it by their attitude toward each other and toward the rest of the family, by their smiles or frowns, by gentleness or harshness, by self-control or lack of it, and by every other manifestation of what lives within them. This is the first instruction the child receives.

As the child grows, Christian parents will instruct it in the life and words of Jesus Christ, and in the Catechism, where God's saving truth is summarized briefly and clearly

And they will teach the child to pray.

Through the additional instruction in the Sunday and weekday schools and the confirmation class, the child is prepared for the act of confirmation.

9. CONFIRMATION

Confirmation rests on God's covenant in Baptism. The God who deals with you in confirmation is He who established His covenant with you in Baptism.

To be confirmed means to be made firm, to be established. It is my faith in God the Father, Son, and Holy Spirit and my decision to serve Him that is being made firm. It is, therefore, God that confirms me. During the preparation I am instructed in God's Word which establishes and confirms my faith and decision. On confirmation day I confess that I forsake the devil and all his works and all his ways, that I believe in God the Father, Son, and Holy Spirit, and that it is my decision to serve Him throughout my whole life. Through the prayer of the congregation with the laying on of the hand of the pastor, and through God's blessing pronounced upon me, God strengthens this my faith and decision.

Confirmation is an act of love and grace on the part of my heavenly Father. It is a privilege and an opportunity to confess my faith before the congregation as I am ready to join in the partaking of the Lord's Supper.

+   +   +

We have completed another, the fourth, lesson in our study of God's way of salvation. In the first lesson, the Ten Commandments, we learned that we are lost and condemned sinners. The Creed made it clear that God sent His Son to die for our sins and to save every one who believes in Jesus Christ. The Lord's Prayer taught us that prayer in Jesus' name is a necessary part of the way of salvation.

In our study of the Sacrament of Baptism, we have now learned that here we have another part of the way of salvation. In Baptism, God made us His children, established His covenant with each individual, and gave us a program for our life.

Prayer:

> O Lord, our little ones to Thee
> In faith and hope we give;
> We know that through this mystery
> Their new-born soul shall live.

Help them to go from strength to strength,
Until, full-grown in Thee,
They come before Thy face at length,
And all Thy glory see. Amen.

(L. H., No. 144, vv. 1 and 3)

QUESTIONS

(To be answered in writing, except 1 and 2)

1. Look up and read in your Bible all the Bible passages quoted in this chapter. Underscore them in your Bible.
2. Be ready to recite the material that is to be memorized.
3. Give three reasons for baptizing infants.
4. Prove from God's Word that baby is a sinner.
5. How do you explain that a new-born baby is a sinner?
6. What does it mean to be children of wrath?
7. State how experience proves that baby is born with a sinful nature.
8. Prove from God's Word that baby needs to be born anew.
9. What good does it do to baptize a child?
10. Give the Biblical answer to the claim that children cannot believe.
11. Who creates faith in Jesus?
12. How would you describe a child's faith?
13. State historical evidences that prove that infant baptism was practiced in the early church. (See footnote.)
14. Why should not baptized children who fall away be re-baptized when they later are converted?
15. How is the spiritual life of children nourished?
16. Who are the children's first teachers?
17. By what means do these teachers instruct the children?
18. What did Jesus command us to teach those whom we baptize?
19. Who is it that confirms the child in confirmation?
20. What is it in the child that needs to be confirmed?
21. By what means is the child confirmed?
22. State the four lessons we have learned in our study of God's way of salvation.

BIBLE STUDY

After reading Col. 2:8-12, state (1) with whom philosophy and vain deceit originate; (2) what is said of Christ in verses 9 and 10; (3) of what the Christians "are made full" (v. 10); (4) when they obtained this fullness; (5) what has taken the place of circumcision; (6) how old the Old Testament boys were when circumcised (see Gen. 17:12 and Luke 2:21); (7) what light this throws on infant Baptism

CHAPTER THIRTY-FOUR

The Sacrament of the Altar

Before we begin our study of the Sacrament of the Altar, we shall devote some space to that part of the Catechism which is headed: Of Confession.

Let us see what the Word of God teaches regarding confession of sins.

1. CONFESSION A PRIVILEGE

Confession is a privilege and a help for struggling souls.

Sometimes a special sin, old or new, is gnawing at the conscience, or the spiritual life is in such confusion that you do not know what to do.

In such cases it will help to tell your trouble to your pastor or some other Christian, in whom you have confidence. You may ask him to absolve you, that is, place his hand upon your head and declare unto you the forgiveness of your sins in the name of the Father and of the Son and of the Holy Spirit.

Confess, therefore, your sins one to another, and pray one for another, that ye may be healed (James 5:16).

Christ has given all His disciples the authority in His name to declare the forgiveness of sins.

Whose soever sins ye forgive, they are forgiven unto them (John 20:23).

In the Lutheran Church confession together with absolution is generally used as preparation for the partaking of the Lord's Supper. This public confession is so worded that all communicants can join. The individual is a part of the group. The laying on of hands upon the heads of the communicants symbolizes that the absolution is personal.

In private confession the individual is alone. He can tell his personal difficulties and receive the brotherly help that he especially needs.

It is of this private confession that the Catechism speaks in the following questions and answers.

2. What Is Confession?
Confession consists of two parts: the one is that we confess our sins; the other, that we receive absolution or forgiveness from the pastor as from God Himself, in no wise doubting, but firmly believing, that our sins are thereby forgiven before God in heaven.

3. What Sins Should We Confess?
Before God we should acknowledge ourselves guilty of all manner of sins, even of those of which we are not aware, as we do in the Lord's Prayer. To the pastor we should confess only those sins which we know and feel in our hearts.

4. What Are Such Sins?
Here examine yourself in the light of the Ten Commandments, whether as father or mother, son or daughter, master or servant, you have been disobedient, unfaithful, slothful, ill-tempered, unchaste, or quarrelsome, or whether you have injured any one by word or deed, stolen, neglected or wasted aught, or done any other evil.

THE SACRAMENT OF THE ALTAR

5. NAMES
In the Bible, this Sacrament is called the Lord's Supper because the Lord instituted it during the Passover Supper (I Cor. 11:20). It is also named the Lord's Table because the bread and wine were placed on a table, the communicants sitting around the table as at a meal (I Cor. 10:21). Finally, the name Communion is derived from I Cor. 10:16. It means fellowship, participation. Christ communes, that is, has fellowship with His guests and they with one another.

The church has added two names. The first is the Sacrament of the Altar. When altars came into use in the churches, the Sacrament was administered at the altar instead of at a table. The second name is the Eucharist, which means thanksgiving.

6. HISTORIC BACKGROUND

Israel's stay in Egypt was at an end. A last terrible stroke from Jehovah would break Pharaoh's resistance and send the people on their way.

But the people of Israel also had a lesson to learn. They were not to be saved because of their worthiness, but because Jehovah would fulfill His promises. They would be set free only if they sought protection behind the sacrificial blood. So they were instructed to kill a lamb for each household and put the blood on the two sideposts and on the lintel of the door leading into the house. The flesh they were to roast and eat with unleavened bread and bitter herbs. They were to be dressed ready for the journey with staff in their hands. When the angel passed through Egypt on his mission of death he would see the blood on the houses of Israel and "pass over" them. Their first-born would not be slain.

In obedient faith Israel did as the Lord said. Behind the blood they were safe, and they could walk out of the land of bondage into God's freedom.

The event was called the Passover and was celebrated annually as the greatest national festival (Ex. 12).

The lamb was a symbol of Christ, who is the true Passover Lamb, and the Lord's Supper is the New Testament Passover meal for God's people.

Our Passover also hath been sacrificed, even Christ (I Cor. 5:7).

7. WHAT THE SACRAMENT IS

What is the sacrament of the altar?

Answer: It is the true body and blood of our Lord Jesus Christ, under the bread and wine, given unto us Christians to eat and to drink, as it was instituted by Christ Himself.

Where is it so written?

Answer: The holy evangelists, Matthew, Mark, and Luke, together with St. Paul, write thus:

Our Lord Jesus Christ, in the night in which He was betrayed, took bread; and when He had given thanks, He brake it and gave it to His disciples, saying, Take, eat; this is My body, which is given for you; this do in remembrance of Me.

154

After the same manner also He took the cup, when He had supped, and when He had given thanks, He gave it to them, saying, Drink ye all of it; this cup is the new testament in My blood, which is shed for you, and for many, for the remission of sins; this do, as often as ye drink of it, in remembrance of Me.

8. IN THE NIGHT IN WHICH HE WAS BETRAYED

Jesus and His disciples were gathered for the festival of the Passover meal. The opening words of John's account of the festival disclose Christ's motive for instituting this Sacrament. "Jesus knowing that His hour was come that He should depart out of this world unto the Father, having loved His own that were in the world, He loved them unto the end" (John 13:1).

Luke quotes the words by which Jesus introduced the Institution of the Sacrament.

With desire I have desired to eat this Passover with you before I suffer (Luke 22:15).

He forgot Himself, and the torture, and the cross of the next day. He even dismissed from His mind the knowledge that Judas would betray Him, the disciples forsake Him, and Peter deny Him. His every thought and desire centered on the disciples and their future. He had it all planned that at this Passover He would give them a new means of grace and a new proof of His love. And He did so in the night in which He was betrayed!

9. HIS BODY—HIS BLOOD

We reject the teaching that the bread and wine are merely signs of Christ's body and blood. Christ's words are plain. "This is My body which is given for you." "This cup is the new testament in My blood." The apostle writes:

The cup of blessing which we bless, is it not a communion of the blood of Christ? The bread which we break, is it not a communion of the body of Christ? (I Cor. 10:16.)

There can be no communion, fellowship between the bread and the wine and the body and blood of Christ unless the body and blood are actually present in the Sacrament.

We also reject the teaching that the bread and wine have been transformed or changed into the body and blood and

155

are no longer bread and wine. The apostle says that there is a communion of the body and blood, as the guests at the Lord's table eat the bread and drink the wine. There is no transformation of the bread and wine.

When the Catechism says that the Sacrament of the Altar is the true body and blood of Christ, it means that it is the actual, real body and blood, not merely signs.

Again we are facing the mystery. We do not understand how Jesus Christ, in the Sacrament, gives us His body and blood. We believe it because He says it. No one can explain it.

10. UNION CAUSED BY CHRIST'S WORD

If we ask how the body and blood of Christ can be in the bread and wine, the answer is that the union is caused by the power of His word. There is no limit to the power of Christ's word in the carrying out of His plan.

As the union between the body and the bread, and the blood and the wine is caused by His word, so the union takes place when the bread and the wine are partaken of as Christ's words are spoken by the pastor. The union does not take place before, nor does it last after the eating and the drinking. The bread that may be left on the plate and the wine that may be left in the cup are only bread and wine.

Prayer:

> I hear Thy voice; Thou bidst me come and rest:
> I come, I kneel, I clasp Thy pierced feet:
> Thou bidst me take my place, a welcome guest
> Among Thy saints, and of Thy banquet eat.
>
> My praise can only breathe itself in prayer.
> My prayer can only lose itself in Thee;
> Dwell Thou for ever in my heart, and there,
> Lord, let me sup with Thee; sup Thou with me. Amen.
>
> (L. H. No. 310, vv. 5 and 6)

QUESTIONS
(To be answered in writing, except 1 and 2)

1. Look up and read in your Bible the Bible passages quoted in this chapter. Underscore them in your Bible.
2. Be ready to recite the material that is to be memorized.
3. What is the purpose of confession?

4. Why is confession a privilege?
5. To whom has Christ given the authority to forgive sin?
6. State the difference between public and private confession.
7. State (1) the Biblical names of the Sacrament of the Altar; (2) the names given by the church.
8. When was the Old Testament Passover instituted?
9. What kind of animal was killed?
10. How was the blood used?
11. State the reason why the blood was so used.
12. What lesson did God teach Israel through the Passover?
13. Explain the relation between the Passover and the Lord's Supper.
14. When did Christ institute the Lord's Supper?
15. How does the apostle John begin his account of what took place that evening?
16. For whom was this Sacrament instituted?
17. What is the Sacrament of the Altar?
18. Why is the word "true" used?
19. Give the reason why we reject the teaching that the bread and wine are merely signs of Christ's body and blood.
20. Why do we reject the teaching that the bread and wine have been transformed into the body and blood of Christ?
21. What causes the union between the bread and wine and the body and blood of Christ?
22. At what moment does the union take place?

BIBLE STUDY

Read Ex. 12, verses 1-14, and verses 43-51.
1. What was the purpose of the killing of the Passover lamb?
2. Why was the blood put on the door posts and the lintel?
3. Compare the following passages and state in what ways the Passover lamb was a type of Christ: Ex. 12:3 and John 1:29; Ex. 12:5 and Luke 3:23 (a one year old lamb is in the prime of life, at thirty a man is in the prime of life); Ex. 2:7 and 13 and I Pet. 1:18-19; Ex. 12:46 and John 19:36.
4. What relation is there between the Passover and the Lord's Supper? (See I Cor. 5:7.)

CHAPTER THIRTY-FIVE

The Sacrament of the Altar: Benefits

We have seen that in the Lord's Supper we eat and drink the body and blood of our Savior Jesus Christ.

1. BENEFITS OF THE SACRAMENT

What is the benefit of such eating and drinking?

Answer: It is pointed out in these words:

Given and shed for you for the remission of sins.

Through these words the remission of sins, life, and salvation are given unto us in the Sacrament; for where there is remission of sins, there is also life and salvation.

God's saving grace is not divided. Where it is, there is the whole of it. Where there is remission of sins, there is also life and salvation.

2. FORGIVENESS OF SIN IN THE SACRAMENT

Christ's body was given and His blood was shed on the cross for you, that is, for your sins. Dying on the cross, He obtained forgiveness of sins for you.

According to His words, His body is in the bread and His blood is in the wine of the Sacrament. It is the body that was given and the blood that was shed on the cross for your sins. Receiving His body and blood, you receive the forgiveness of your sins. It is a gift that His body and blood always bring. His body and blood cannot be separated from the forgiveness of sins.

When Christ says that this cup is the new testament He means that this cup is forgiveness of sins. (Chap. Thirty-four, 7.) His blood is in the cup, and forgiveness of sins is in His blood. You cannot drink His blood without having the forgiveness of your sins given to you. You may not accept it, but the gift is in the Sacrament.

Christ cannot give you and me the forgiveness of our sins in a more personal, direct, and emphatic manner.

3. NOT EATING AND DRINKING, BUT THE WORD

How can bodily eating and drinking produce such great benefits?

Answer: The eating and drinking, indeed, do not produce them, but the words:

Given and shed for you for the remission of sins.

For besides the bodily eating and drinking, these words are the chief thing in the Sacrament; and he who believes them, has what they say and declare, the remission of sins.

4. HIS WORD—MY FAITH

Forgiveness of sins, and life and salvation are always in the Lord's Supper, not because of my faith, but because of Christ's word. These gifts are there whether or not I believe it. However, these gifts do not benefit me unless I believe what Christ says. It is by faith in the words, *Given and shed for you for the remission of sins,* that forgiveness and life and salvation become my possession

5. I NEED THE PERSONAL GUARANTY

Why do I need forgiveness of my sins in the Sacrament as long as I live in daily forgiveness for Christ's sake? By giving me His body and blood, Christ assures me personally that my sins are forgiven. I need this repeated assurance, for I am so unworthy and sinful and so full of doubt.

The truth that my sins are forgiven cannot be too much impressed upon me. Often I find it very difficult to believe. But all doubts must disappear in the face of such words and such gifts.

And I am glad and thankful

6. WORTHY GUESTS

Who, then, receives the Sacrament worthily?

Answer: Fasting and bodily preparation are indeed a good outward discipline, but he is truly worthy and well prepared who believes these words:

Given and shed for you for the remission of sins.

But he who does not believe these words or who doubts them, is unworthy and unprepared; for the words "for you" require truly believing hearts.

7. FAITH AND FAITH ALONE

Why is it that faith and faith alone makes us worthy guests at the Lord's Table?

The answer is that in the Sacrament Christ comes to give gifts to us and not to find out what we can do. He wants us to accept His gifts that He may gladden and strengthen us. This He can do only when we believe the words, *Given and shed for you for the remission of sins.*

Fasting is an ancient custom. The communicants did not eat breakfast the day they went to the Communion, and at times they did not even eat supper the day before. It may be good discipline, but adds nothing to our worthiness. Hypocrites may fast just as readily as honest believers.

8. MISUSING THE SACRAMENT

The apostle warns against misusing the Sacrament. *For he that eateth and drinketh, eateth and drinketh judgment unto himself, if he discern not the body* (I Cor. 11:29).

As an expression of their fellowship, the Christians at Corinth came together for their evening meals, the so-called love feasts. They finished the meal by partaking of the Lord's Supper.

Soon disorder crept in. The rich would gather around their choice food and wine and overindulge, till they were actually drunk. The poor were left with whatever food they were able to bring, and they became envious of the rich. In this condition they would partake of the Sacrament.

The apostle says they did not discern the body. That is, they did not pay any attention to the fact that in the Sacrament they received the body of Christ. The Sacrament was only a ceremony that finished the meal. They ate unworthily and brought judgment upon themselves.

He is an unworthy guest at the Lord's Table who goes thoughtlessly, does not repent of his sins, and does not come to the Sacrament in order to receive forgiveness and strength to live a Christ-like life. For he does not really believe these words: *Given and shed for you for the remission of sins.*

9. PROVING MYSELF

Let a man prove himself, and so let him eat of the bread and drink of the cup (I Cor. 11:28).

The proving consists in asking myself, "Do I believe that in the Sacrament I receive the body and blood of Christ? Do I need it in order to become more firmly assured of the forgiveness of my sins? Do I partake of the Sacrament in order to be strengthened to a truer and fuller service of my Lord and Savior?"

If my answer is a yes, then I am a worthy guest, however unworthy I am in my own eyes

10. HOW OFTEN

How often we should go to the Lord's Table is left to individual need and opportunity.

Christ's words, "This do, as oft as ye drink it," have been taken to imply a frequent partaking of the Lord's Supper. So the first Christians understood the words. They went to the Lord's Table every day (see Acts 2:46-47). It was to them a festal meal, that gladdened and strengthened them. Christian experience proves that a frequent use of the Sacrament strengthens our faith in Christ and inspires to holy living.

11. IN REMEMBRANCE OF ME

Christ said, *"This do, as oft as ye drink it, in remembrance of Me."*

We cannot be worthy guests at the Lord's Supper without remembering Christ and His love. It is Christ that meets me in the Sacrament—He who suffered and died that I may live.

12. A TESTIMONY

As oft as ye eat this bread, and drink the cup, ye proclaim the Lord's death till He come (I Cor. 11:26).

At the Lord's Table I am a witness for Christ. I testify that I build my salvation on the crucified and risen Lord Jesus and on nothing else. He is my Savior, my Lord, and my God.

Prayer:

O Jesus, blessed Lord, to Thee
My heartfelt thanks forever be,
Who hast so lovingly bestowed
On me Thy body and Thy blood. Amen.

(L. H. No. 155, v. 1)

QUESTIONS

(To be answered in writing, except 1 and 2)

1. Look up and read in your Bible the Bible passages quoted in this chapter. Underscore them in your Bible.
2. Be ready to recite the material that is to be memorized.
3. State in your own words the benefit of eating and drinking the Lord's body and blood.
4. Why does the Lord's Supper always bring forgiveness of sins?
5. What is needed on our part in order that this forgiveness may be ours?
6. Explain the words, "This cup is the new testament."
7. What causes forgiveness of sin to be a part of the Sacrament?
8. Why does a child of God need the forgiveness given in the Sacrament?
9. State the reason why faith alone makes us worthy guests at the Lord's Table.
10. Describe the disorder at the love feasts at Corinth (I Cor. 11: 17-34).
11. Who is an unworthy guest?
12. Why should we prove ourselves when going to the Lord's Table?
13. How should we prove ourselves?
14. Give reasons why we often should partake of the Lord's Supper.
15. How often did the first Christians go to the Lord's Table?
16. Why should we remember Christ when partaking of the Sacrament?
17. What testimony do we bear when we are guests at the Lord's Table?

BIBLE STUDY

Read Matthew 26:17-30 and state (1) why the Passover is called the unleavened bread (see Ex. 12:15); (2) the meaning of "My time is at hand"; (3) what Jesus did after taking the bread; (4) what Jesus said when He gave the disciples the bread; (5) what He did when He had taken the cup; (6) what He said when He gave them the cup; (7) the meaning of "the blood of the covenant"; (8) in what way He gave them the blood of the covenant; (9) the meaning of the new wine in v. 29 (it refers to Pentecost); (10) why they sang a hymn of thanksgiving (Ps. 118).

CHAPTER THIRTY-SIX

Old Truths and New Experiences

In the opening paragraph of Chapter One I learned that, *It is God's will that all men be saved and come to the knowledge of the truth* (I Tim. 2:4).

I have studied God's way of salvation as taught in the Bible and presented in Luther's Small Catechism.

1. THE FIVE LESSONS

In the Ten Commandments God taught me how I should live as His child. As I learned to see myself in the light of God's will, He convinced me that I have been a very disobedient child. The question arose, How can I be saved from God's judgment? This was the first lesson.

The second lesson or the Creed gave the answer. God, my heavenly Father, sent His Son to save sinners, and the Holy Spirit leads me to trust in the forgiveness of my sins for Christ's sake. At the same time the Spirit creates love to Jesus Christ and desire to serve Him.

The third lesson I learned in the study of the Lord's Prayer. "God tenderly encourages us . . . that we may boldly and confidently come to Him in prayer." If I do not pray, the Holy Spirit can not do His saving work in me.

The study of the Sacrament of Baptism furnished the fourth lesson. In His work to save man from sin, God enters into covenants with His people. In Baptism God established

His covenant with me. He gave me a new heart and a program for my life.

The fifth lesson became clear in the study of the Sacrament of the Altar. In His loving care, Jesus Christ instituted a festal meal for the people of the new covenant. He gives His body and blood to each communicant and in and with the body and blood He gives the forgiveness of sins. Thus the Lord warms the hearts of His friends and strengthens their struggling faith.

2. CHRIST THE WAY

The five lessons do not teach five ways of salvation. There is only one way. *I am the way, and the truth, and the life,* Jesus said (John 14:6).

I. Christ is God's way to man.

God deals with man through Christ.

God gave the law through the Son, as He did everything else through Him (see Heb. 1:2). In the law Jesus Christ speaks. Christ, the Son is the judge, and He shall judge according to His word (see Chap. Nineteen, 4). When Christ said, "I say unto you" (Matt. 5:22, etc.), the highest authority spoke.

Jesus Christ revealed the Father. He redeemed me, and He and the Father sent the Holy Spirit. My prayers are in Christ's name. He instituted the Sacraments, and the Word and the Sacraments are means of grace because of Him.

Truly, Christ is God's way to man.

II. Christ is man's way to God.

No one cometh unto the Father but by Me (John 14:6).

When I use the means of grace, when I pray in Jesus' name, when I trust Jesus Christ as my Savior, when I love and serve Him and my neighbor for His sake, and when I confess my sins and receive the forgiveness that He has provided, then I am traveling in God's way of salvation.

Yes, Christ is man's way to God.

3. NEW EXPERIENCES

I am soon to be confirmed and shall, for the first time, be a guest at the Lord's Table. These will be new and, I pray, rich and joyous experiences. Christ, my Savior and

Friend, will confirm me, and He sets His table with food for my soul.

Confirmation and the first Communion are not graduating exercises. They are the very opposite. Through them Christ, my Lord, will introduce me to a richer and more fruitful life.

But I have to face the issue. Faith in Jesus Christ is a personal matter. No one can believe for me, neither can any one be a Christian in my stead. So, the question can not be avoided. Have I given my heart to Christ? If I have not, my confirmation will be merely a stirring ceremony of little or no spiritual value. Yes, it may even be harmful. And the Lord's Table is not for me.

On the other hand, if Christ is the Lord of my heart, then it will be a privilege publicly to rededicate myself to Him and to sup with Him as He will sup with me in the Sacrament.

4. PRACTICAL HELPS

What will happen after my confirmation? Whatever may happen, I shall not fear. I am not alone.

I trust Christ and the Holy Spirit to keep me. When instituting the Sacrament of Baptism, Christ promised, *Lo, I am with you always, even unto the end of the world* (Matt. 28:20).

He keeps the promises of His covenant.

Then I shall attend church services and the Lord's Table. I shall join a Bible class and take part in Christian young people's work. I shall seek the fellowship of the communion of saints.

I shall also read my Bible, especially the passages I have underscored, and I shall underscore others as I go along. And I shall pray. I may get myself a book of daily devotions, and at times I shall reread my confirmation book.

I have made my decision. I will serve the Lord.

5. SPIRITUAL ADVENTURES

During the course we have discussed many sides of the Christian life of which I have very little experience. The life with Christ is to me at present largely an unexplored country.

165

I know something about my sinfulness, but I begin to realize that I have possibilities for evil that some day may shock me. I know that Christ is faithful and forgiving, but the discussions have impressed upon me the conviction that I shall find Him faithful and forgiving beyond my most daring expectations. My book has had a great deal to say about God's grace. At the same time it has been made clear, that the riches of God's grace in Christ (Eph. 1:7) will be a constant source of happy surprises in years to come.

My spiritual horizon has expanded during these months. Still, I realize that this is only a beginning. Christ speaks about "My joy" being in you and your joy being made full. Clearly, these words point to a world of glorious experiences. The apostle wants to know, that is, to experience, the power of Christ's resurrection and the fellowship of His suffering (Phil. 3:10). Truly the future with Christ promises great spiritual adventures.

I begin to understand another thing. There is no joy in being a half-hearted follower of Christ. A divided heart is a spiritual tragedy.

If ye keep My commandments, ye shall abide in My love; even as I have kept My Father's commandments, and abide in His love. These things have I spoken unto you, that My joy may be in you, and that your joy may be made full (John 15:10-11).

A new commandment I give unto you, that ye love one another; even as I have loved you, that ye also love one another (John 13:34).

6. PRESSING ON

And so my face is set toward a future with Christ.

One thing I do, forgetting the things which are behind, and stretching forward to the things which are before, I press on toward the goal unto the prize of the high calling of God in Christ Jesus (Phil. 3:13-14).

Be thou faithful unto death, and I will give thee the crown of life (Rev. 2:10).

Indeed I will press on toward the goal, trusting Christ.

Peace I leave with you; My peace I give unto you. . . . Let not your heart be troubled, neither let it be fearful (John 14:27).

Run the straight race through God's good grace,
Lift up thine eyes, and seek His face;
Life with its way before us lies,
Christ is the path, and Christ the prize.

(L. H. No. 258, v. 2)

Prayer:

O help us, dear Father, and Christ, Thou the Son,
That gladly our course we may finish!
And Thou, Holy Spirit, Thou comforting One,
Thy love in our hearts so replenish,
That we by Thy might
May fight the good fight,
Till won is the crown everlasting. Amen.

(L. H. No. 51, v. 2)

QUESTIONS

(To be answered in writing, except 1 and 2)

1. Look up and read in your Bible the Bible passages quoted in this chapter. Underscore them in your Bible.
2. Be ready to recite the material that is to be memorized.
3. What plan have we followed in the study of God's way of salvation?
4. How did we get five lessons?
5. State the five lessons.
6. How many ways of salvation are there according to God's Word?
7. Who is the way of salvation?
8. When do we travel in the way of salvation?
9. State the purpose of your confirmation and of your first Communion.
10. What issue do you have to face as you approach your confirmation?
11. List the practical helps that you need after confirmation.
12. Why is the life with Christ largely an unexplored country to you?
13. What new experiences may be in store for you?
14. Why is a divided heart a spiritual tragedy?
15. What is the goal of God's high calling in Christ?
16. How do we press on toward the goal?
17. Why may I press on in hope of reaching the goal?
(See II Tim. 1:12 and Phil. 1:6.)